THE GREAT AMERICAN CONTRACTOR

Special Thanks

Special thanks to all of the people who inspired the words on these pages and without whose stories I would not have had a damn thing to say on this subject. Thank you to all of my friends, Chris, Vanessa, Amy, I'm probably missing someone, for reading the manuscript and giving me invaluable feedback and support. A truly special thanks to my wife, Melissa, who never questioned me for undertaking this time consuming and likely fruitless venture. Without her support I doubtful would have had the confidence to finish this project. I'd also like to thank the great clients I've had over the years who more than made up for the loser clients I've had. A very special thanks, though, to the loser clients. Even if I sell just one copy of this book, it will be in some part because of the stories of struggle that I have told on these pages. Without those terrible clients, the book would be void of authenticity and not worth the pulp it is printed on, so thank you losers. And finally a super special thanks to anyone who is actually reading the special thanks section. If you are enthusiastic enough to be reading the special thanks section, then you are a really good person, and I commend you.

FIRST EDITION

Published by Kelly Cowan January 2022

Designed and Typeset by - Greg Horton

For Lucky Boy, always remember: safety second.

CHAPTER 1

"Opportunity is missed by most people because it is dressed in overalls and looks like work."
—Thomas Edison

Love your job and you'll never work a day in your life—or so they say. In my experience this is *mostly* true, but I've also found that loving your job is much easier said than done. I love designing homes and then seemingly conjuring those designs out of thin air; I mean really and truly fucking love it. But I usually can't tell whether I am an architect, a contractor, a degenerate riverboat gambler, or just a broken man in an abusive relationship—a battered husband sticking with my woman no matter what cruelty she dishes out. I am deeply devoted to what I do for a living, even though it has literally almost killed me. I still love it. I think about building all day, every day. On the weekends I design, build, repair, and improve my own home or do favors for friends on their homes. At night I dream building. My contractor buddy Matt asks me every once in a while, "What would you do tomorrow if you won the lottery today?" and my answer is always the same: "I'd go to work." Matt always says, "Yeah, me too."

I am sitting here editing this thing at 5:00 a.m. on a freezing cold Sunday in the dark—trying not to wake my family—not because I want to boast about how cool builders are, and conversely, not to bitch and moan about how hard contracting is. I'm really here just to brag about all the ways I have saved the day in some extremely tricky situations. Just kidding, I'm actually not trying to talk to you about me at all, although I guess that is inevitably the form this will take. I am writing down this drivel to share with you, dear reader, a story about the clandestine group of men (mostly) who build the world around you. I am here to tell a story about real winners, and of course, absolute losers. I am here to pull back the curtain—ever so slightly—on your built environment.

I spend most days operating in a noisy, dirty, rude, and often dangerous world where seemingly by ancient tradition, only the otherwise unemployable are employed. I am sure my fellow tradesmen will identify with this mysterious and harsh place that I am describing: where bravery is rewarded with the silent nodding endorsement of your peers, and most guys have endless horror story credentials ready to deploy at a moment's notice to prove it to you. I am writing this book for the plumbers, electricians, roofers, and day laborers who in order to make homes happen have to wade through human shit, get shocked, fall off roofs, and just plain suffer, respectively. I hope they read this and get some satisfaction out of their daily grind being sensationalized to the extent that a hack writer like myself is capable. But I am also writing this to share with the average person how the sausage that you call home is made. I want you to know that the guy in the next lane driving a beater pickup that is overloaded with plywood and has marijuana smoke billowing out of the windows might actually be a gifted tradesman, and is for damn sure not as low as you can go on the tradesperson totem pole—I mean, he is driving an actual pickup truck for fuck's sake.

I guess there is going to be a bit of swearing in this book, and I apologize in advance for the rest of the swear words that are surely on their way. I will do my best not to slip into jobsite lingo too much, but it is hard for me to tell some stories without the proper colorized language to set the scene. Who knows, maybe in the second edition, I'll include a glossary of terms.

Building a home or any other kind of building is not for the faint of heart. It's not easy, it's not safe, and there is a fine line between making a profit and building someone else's house with your own money. The men and women who choose a life in the trades have chosen a life of freedom. They have chosen to work in a world that few outsiders will understand or admire. Those who never chose that life, but ended up there anyways, are included here as well. I want to apologize in advance to any of my fellow tradesfolk who would prefer not to open the curtain; I understand the desire to remain anonymous, but whatever gripe they may have, they must also admit that my accounting is authentic. If all goes to plan, this collection of stories, observations, and plain old rants will give the average person a brief glimpse into the netherworld of the Great American Contractor.

CHAPTER 2

"When we build, let us think that we build forever." —John Ruskin

I may as well start in the beginning—my beginning anyways. I was born December 12, 1978, and that was the day my twenty-five-year-old dad named his business "Cowan and Son Construction." By the time I could walk, I was already a pro at bending nails. My dad would set me up in his wood shop with a block of wood, a handful of nails, and a hammer and turn me loose. According to him, I would spend hours banging on those nails, bending them, straightening them back out, and hammering them some more. I guess a career in the trades was inevitable.

It's funny that for all the time I spent in his noisy workshop as a boy I never got used to loud noises. I remember leaving the shop and sleeping in the front seat of Maynard, my dad's '53 Dodge flatbed, when he was running the loudest of equipment. Most of the time that I am on a jobsite these days, I have a pair of shop-phones sitting on my head just above my ears waiting to be called into action at the first sign of someone starting up a saw or plugging in an air compressor. My dad is hard of hearing, as are a lot of old contractors, and I am trying my best not to end up in the same state.

The noise of the loud saws terrified me back then in my dad's shop, and I have yet to really get used to it. My own four-month-old son has apparently inherited that same aversion to loud noises. I can barely open my mouth without scaring the bejesus out of him—of course, if you asked my wife she would let you know that I am (ironically) quite a loud person. His inherited aversion to loudness hasn't stopped me from taking him to work with me. Of course he has his own pair of shop-phones for hearing protection, so I take him to my jobs and he just sleeps through all manner of cacophony. UPDATE: My son is becoming a loud person too. He is thirteen months now and has figured out that screaming is an effective means of communication. He's clearly a genius.

During the time when I was growing up in my dad's shop, he was the local artist-builder-historical-restoration-guy in the town of Ferndale on the north coast of California. He gained a reputation for doing top quality work, and became known for his historically accurate doors and windows—not to mention his restoration projects at large. Eventually he would become a teacher of Historic Millwork and Practices at the College of the Redwoods. He always put a high value on well-made things, and he always took his time with everything he did. He especially valued the artistic and skilled craftsmanship that was ubiquitous in older buildings, and if you want to make his blood boil tell him you are replacing your old, drafty, single-pane windows with new, energy efficient, vinyl windows. Even writing those words down makes me feel like I am committing some sort of building blasphemy.

He is right, though. Your drafty old windows are the most historically significant thing on your house; change them and you go straight to hell—at least that's what I was brought up to believe. No other feature on a building has the same significance as a window; they are like the eyes of a building in that way. If you were to change out the eyeballs on your face with some cheap, energy-efficient knock-offs, you would regret it, right? Fortunately for the world my dad is here to create dual pane, energy efficient, *and* historically accurate replacement windows. You can go to his website that I set up for him and see for yourself: danecowan.com. Tell your friends.

My dad was a terrific teacher, both to me and his students who loved him with all their hearts. He taught his students the way he taught me: with love and patience, and always with attention to detail. This attention to detail meant that in his career he always did high quality work, but it also meant that he cost a lot to hire, and not everyone wants to pay a guy like my dad to take his time—especially if they think they are an expert (most everyone does). Most people think that every project—no matter how complex—should somehow be done quicker, better, and cheaper. If you hang around lumber yards (and who doesn't?), before long you will hear someone say something to the effect of, "Cheap, Quick, and Good. You can have two out of the three, but you can't have all three." It's funny because it's true. Then again, it's actually not funny because it is so often the source of grief for clients and builders alike. You can have work done cheap and fast (but it will be a piece of garbage), or you can have quality and have it right away (but it will cost you), or you can have quality and maybe not cost you an arm and a leg, but you will have it when you have it (stop calling me). If you only have one of the three, it really better be the good.

I think my dad always tried to hover in the quality, quick, but not cheap range, but he didn't always provide the timeliness leg of the tripod and it got him into some hot water from time to time. In his defense, I think we all would like to be so valued for the quality of our work that we would be paid handsomely and no one would care how long it took. The best services and the best places in the world are afforded this freedom. If you go to the French Laundry restaurant in Napa you know you are going to pay and you are going be sitting there for four to six hours (not to mention the eight months you already waited just to get a table). If you are having brain surgery you're not going to be laying on the table saying, "Hey Doc, I'm paying good money here, how much longer is this going to take? I was hoping to beat traffic on the way home." Of course we don't value builders in the same way we do our surgeons, or even our chefs for that matter, but more on that later.

Since before I can even remember, I was using the tools in my dad's shop and learning how to fasten pieces of wood together. When you really break things down to their simplest elements that is all building is: assembling two or more things together to create three-dimensional space. Learning that at a young age was, for me, comparable to learning the piano for many musicians. The piano is laid out in a way that makes musical theory easier to understand. I'm not a trained musician, but from what I have seen and experienced on a very basic level, there is something about the layout of the piano that makes other instruments easier to wrap your head around. The same was true for me learning how to put two pieces of wood together at a young age; it made it easier to understand other pursuits in three-dimensionality. I think that is why I have a knack for sewing. When you break sewing down to its essence it is just putting two or more two-dimensional pieces of fabric together to create something new in three dimensions. I would bet any builder could learn to sew or to weld or you name the assembly task with very little effort. Whether you are building a bridge or a birdhouse, it all starts the same way: with individual parts coming together with more parts to create something bigger and more complex. I know—pretty mind blowing.

My dad is not only gifted at putting things together, but he is a wiz at taking them apart. My cousin Rooker loves telling the story about coming out to visit from Rochester, NY, and helping my dad build a big beautiful piece of furniture. It was so big, in fact, it didn't fit through the front door of the house they were delivering it to. So, my dad simply cut it in half to make it fit, but it still didn't fit, so he had to cut it in half again. My cousin was amazed that my dad could do that, and then reassemble it with none ever being the wiser. That's talent. That's also a classic case of "cut it twice, and it's still too short."

Despite all the noise, some of my fondest memories were of working in my dad's shop. Any time I wanted to build something, he would just say yes and direct me to the right materials and tools. I remember one time wanting to build a crossbow and he helped me figure it out. He didn't do it for me—he just pointed me in the right direction and let me struggle through the engineering problems. I tried to come up with a trigger mechanism, but it never really worked right and the PVC pipe that I thought of using for the springy bow part broke before long, so by all accounts the crossbow was a failure—but it was fun just trying to figure it out. Most parents would probably shy away from letting their nine-year-old build a medieval weapon, but I think my dad's intuition was that the value of building some complex thing purely from scratch far outweighed the risk of me murdering someone. He was like that with pretty much whatever I wanted to create.

"Birdhouse?"

"Yes."

"Hay fort?"

"Absolutely."

"Half-pipe?"

"You bet."

"Pipe bomb?"

"Uh...let's talk about that one." He had to draw the line somewhere I guess. My dad never taught me how to make a pipe bomb, but he did used to have a copy of *The Anarchist Cookbook* lying around. Then one day it wasn't on the bookshelf anymore. Again, I guess he had to draw the line somewhere.

My dad also taught me how to work—as in the protestant work ethic way of working where hard work is its own reward—and when I was tasked with a job by a relative or a friend of the family, I always worked hard and got compliments. It felt good to do a job and see it through to completion. I think one thing young people are missing out on today is the joy of doing a horrible, grueling job from start to finish. There are too many reasons not to have to work today if you are a kid. It's easy to keep kids busy with devices and video games so you don't have to send them outside to keep them occupied. It's too easy to worry about them *going* outside. And worst of all, it's easy to worry about them liking you. So you end up not sending them out to clean the gutters, or mow the lawn, or over to Uncle Leroy's house to help him build his deck because you know they won't like it and they won't like you for making them do it, and they could get hurt anyways—so why not just stay inside and play video games. I benefited from being made to do work at a young age, and it taught me the value of work itself. Of course I didn't like doing it, but I learned how to work. I learned how to put my head down and do a job without worrying about my own comfort, or what I was going to gain from the work. What I was taught was just *how* to work, and eventually I learned that girls found calloused hands sexy, and honestly, that still motivates me today.

Ironically one of the worst jobs I ever worked was also one of the cleanest and easiest. My mom knew someone who managed the Hallmark store in the mall and needed some holiday help (I know, I throw up in my mouth a little every time I read that line). I was responsible for basically stocking shelves, but because I liked to work hard and fast I quickly stocked all that needed stocking and was soon looking for more tasks. The manager was impressed with my work ethic and told my mom that I was the best employee she ever had. My motivation at that job was to get to the end of the day as quickly as possible. I knew instinctually that by putting my head down and working, the time would pass more quickly than if I were just staring at the clock. To this day I can't go within one hundred feet of the mall during the holidays, and only since my son was born have I begun to enjoy Christmas music again.

My mom will argue that I used to hate to work. She loves to tell how she could never pay me to do any work around the house. This was true, but probably had more to do with our relationship than anything else. When given a job to do at someone else's house, I always learned how to do it efficiently. If I had a job to do, the desire to complete the job quickly was in itself enough to motivate me. My uncle Jim knew this and recruited me for jobs at a young age. As early as maybe nine years old, I was doing basic carpentry for Jim out at his plot on Ruth Lake. In terms of my building education, I graduated from my dad's elementary school and began attending Uncle Jim's Preparatory right about then.

CHAPTER 3

"Why worry about doing something you love?
Figure out what the opportunity is. Find a thing,
get good at it, learn to love it later."
—Mike Rowe

Typical of Uncle Jim, he was always trying (and often succeeded) to get high-level work out of cheap (or in my case free) labor. His philosophy was that he could teach just about anyone to do just about anything. He wouldn't always get the finest results, but he always got a pretty good job for way less than if he hired a professional–and because he wasn't paying much for the work, he could afford to do things over and over until he got the results he wanted. Uncle Jim has a philosophy for life that is outside of any conceivable box. I was the unexpected beneficiary from his outside-the-box professionalism. I ended up learning a lot from Uncle Jim at a young age, and I did it all because I was a true believer; I soaked up Uncle Jimisms like a sponge. While I liked the praise I would overhear him giving me, I think I mostly loved working for Jim because I knew I was being bestowed with some ancient wisdom.

My uncle Jim was born in 1942 in the coal town of Wheeling, WV, and grew up just across the Ohio River in Powhatan, OH. Grandfather and his father were coal miners who would both die from the black lung. Jim's dad died when Jim was only fifteen. Jim's uncle was the local handyman, and from the time Jim was a young boy his dad would make him wake up early in the morning, or even at times in the middle of the night, to go with his uncle to fix what needed fixing in their town. Jim learned a little bit about a lot of things from his uncle, and he had that rare personality where he wanted to fully absorb everything he was ever taught. He retained everything his uncle taught him like a savant, and he remembered just about everything he was ever exposed to, which came in handy for me later on when I would call Jim to get me out of any number of fixes I found myself in.

Later, Jim joined the Navy and worked as an electronics technician on the submarine the USS *Cubera* (SS-347). Jim was so well-versed in how everything worked on the submarine—from electronics to hydraulics, rudder to torpedo tubes—that if all hell were to break loose on the sub, he could effectively take command from the captain until the crisis was averted. Jim's tales of adventure on the submarine were ridiculous, and it strikes me that the sailors on his sub were not expected to conduct themselves in a very "military" manner. This was especially so in the 1960s when submarines were diesel-powered, and not the giant technological marvels they are today. The 1960s sub had its own rules and codes of conduct, and probably deserves a book of its own. Where a sailor on an aircraft carrier or a destroyer might get arrested and thrown in the brig for being drunk and disorderly, the Clandestine Service were never there in the first place, and so were simply escorted back to their ship. Uncle Jim was especially immune to normal disciplinary action due to his special status as Guy-in-Charge-When-All-Hell-Breaks-Loose, so he took full advantage. Jim's uniform of choice on the sub was a hoodie, cut-off jean shorts, and cowboy boots.

I must have been about ten years old when I stopped being scared of Uncle Jim; at least enough to start seeing him for the genius he was. For all his skills and extraordinary abilities he was never what you would call a people person. Not that he didn't know how—he could pour on the charm when he wanted to, but I guess he just never really wanted to.

"Hey Jim, do you want to hold the baby?"

"I bet that baby has as much interest in me as I do in it," would be the standard response.

So, around ten years old must have been when I started

mining Jim for information. It was always my great pleasure to be stuck in the car with Uncle Jim. "How does a battery work? How does a water pump work? How does internal combustion work? How does [fill in the blank] work?" He always knew the answer to my questions and I soaked it up. When it came to building, Jim knew just about everything in that department as well. One of my first actual jobs in construction was helping him rebuild his son's restaurant that had burned down in a fire caused by an improperly installed water heater. Within the first week on that job he had me doing framing, plumbing, electrical, and a perennial favorite, outsmarting the building inspector.

Once, when I was a sophomore in high school, Jim had me and a friend out to Ruth Lake to help him build the foundation for his cabin. We dug holes and mixed concrete on a steep hillside in some of the hardest and rockiest ground I've ever encountered. The weather that weekend was miserable—cold and rainy—but I wasn't going to let the opportunity to get towed behind the boat on inflatable inner tubes pass me by no matter how frozen and wet I was at the end of the day. After that trip, Jim always talked about how impressed he was that I worked so hard that weekend. He was pretty much a dick to me while we were working, but he was very complimentary afterwards. Jim worked me and my friend like we were a pair of pack mules. He knew we didn't know shit about building, but that was no excuse. He expected us to do things right, and when we didn't he got pissed and corrected us. He expected us to work like men, and when the work was finally done he treated us like men, albeit men who wanted to go inter-tubing behind a boat in freezing-ass weather.

...

My work ethic—or maybe a better way to say it is my love for work—I believe I owe largely to the two aforementioned men: Uncle Jim and my dad. Both were great teachers, but sit in stark contrast to each other. My dad is a man who takes his time with everything. When teaching me how to do something he would be painstaking in his demonstration of how to use even the simplest tools. My dad's method of teaching was like this: first he would describe the task to you, then he would use a drawing to further explain how the different steps worked, and then he would show you how to do it himself, and he would do it so much that it was almost entirely complete before he let you take over. I was always saying, "I got it, I got it, I GOT IT!" I think it actually was a smart way to teach because there was very little chance of you fucking it up at the point you would take over (because it was practically finished) and it would really bolster your confidence in being able to replicate the task. Uncle Jim's method would be to let a novice try, fail, curse, and then repeat quickly so you'd get it done before the guy who actually knew what he was doing.

I learned to put things together in my dad's shop, and I saw how he valued quality and taking one's time. That taking one's time part never really rubbed off on me—at least it hasn't yet. From Uncle Jim I learned to always look for a quicker or more efficient way to get the job done—sometimes, admittedly, to my detriment. Even something as simple as filling a wheelbarrow full of trash and wheeling it to a dumpster. There must be a more efficient method! If I see a guy, particularly a young guy, walking across a jobsite with nothing in his hands, I will usually say something to the effect of, "You are eventually going to have to carry something to your truck, do it now and save me some money please." If there is a quicker way to do something I will always at least give it a try. Some critics might describe this quicker way of doing things with the judgmental term "shortcut," but I prefer the big flattering word "expediency." After all, if the same quality of work can be done with less physical work, or with less bullshitting, grab-assing, phone-fondling, then why wouldn't you strive for that? And if I can find a shortcut that truly yields the same results as the long way around, then a shortcut I will take.

As much as my dad was an artist, my mom too fancied herself an artist, and both of them fostered in me a deep love for creating art. I was constantly making crafty things as a kid and my favorite way to spend my time was drawing. My favorite thing to draw was war scenes: war vehicles, guns, bombs, explosions—never much death, but always destruction. My second favorite thing to draw, though, was houses. I guess I had a yin and yang thing going on then. I actually had always said from a young age that I wanted to be an architect. It seems like I am continually hearing stories about little kids knowing what they are going to be when they grow up, and I think I knew. I never actually became an architect (yet...hoping for that honorary degree) but I often describe myself as an unlicensed architect (read: shortcut?). In any case, I am now doing for a living what I thought I'd be doing when I was a kid looking into the future—I design and build beautiful buildings.

My first formal training in designing and building came in high school when I took a drafting class taught by our woodshop teacher. I never took woodshop, probably because I grew up in a woodshop, but the other reason could have been that our woodshop teacher was missing about four and a half fingers. Nothing says stay away from the table saw like the sight of missing fingers. But I figured drafting class couldn't be that dangerous. The worst that could happen in drafting was getting stabbed with a pencil—which incidentally I was, and I still have the graphite in my hand to show for it.

Upon graduating high school, I think I thought I might want to be a sports agent or something to do with the sports world—seems silly now, but I love sports and I think Jerry

Maguire came out right around the time I graduated from high school. As soon as I transferred from junior college to UC San Diego, however, I found Urban Studies and Planning, and I knew that that was the place I was supposed to be. I loved every minute of my USP education. While in hindsight I might have benefitted more from an architecture degree or a degree in fine art, I still think if I had it all to do over again, I would be hard pressed not to study the exact same thing. Urban Studies meant studying the built environment, and was akin to studying the design of cities at large. Every city could be seen as a collective art installation of the highest magnitude coordinated by an entire population generations at a time, albeit without the majority of people involved having any awareness whatsoever of their participation in said project. That being said some cities have been "designed" beautifully, and some design sucks, therefore so do some cities.

Take San Francisco as an example of the former. San Francisco is one of the most beautiful cities in America, but it was not planned from the beginning to look and feel as it does now. It evolved over time to accommodate the whims of the citizens, the various modes of transportation, and the powers that be. It grew out of nothing in 1849 to twenty-five thousand people in one year. Like most charming towns, it began in an era before zoning regulations and grew organically, guided only by the market. The tug of war between the Slow-Growth movement, No-Growth movement, and powerful developers pushed and pulled the city into the shape it is in now. Sprinkle in a couple of earthquakes, a fire, some weird lawsuits, and voilà! You got yourself one of the most beloved cities in the world. Even if you hate San Francisco (I myself have fallen out of love with the place), you have to admit it is one of the most beautiful cities in existence today.

Luckily for humans, a city created during the time when the horse was the most reliable form of transportation was by default an intimate place. Therefore, cities like Philadelphia, New York, Chicago, and San Francisco are really nice places to be (on good days). On the other hand, some cities like Columbia, MD (lived there), Rohnert Park, CA (lived near there), or Houston, TX (ironically, thinking of moving there), which were completely "planned" from the very beginning totally fail at being beloved, or iconic, or even comfortable cities. Columbia and Rohnert Park, more so than Houston, were literally designed to be really nice places to live, and they both miss the mark completely—that pretty much tells you all you need to know about planning. What I learned in my studies is that planning does not guarantee beautiful cities any more than a lack of planning. It's actually immaterial because development is what drives the form of a city, and the best you can do from an Urban Studies and Planning perspective is observe what works and what doesn't, and then report on it in a snarky manner. Great cities happen through luck, violence, lack of oversight, and not from smart people's best intentions. Planning a perfect city is only possible in the Sim City video game (even then not easy).

If you want to be a city planner (different from a planner of cities), then Urban Studies and Planning might not be for you—at least not at UCSD at the time I was there. USP was more a study in why cities were the way they were, what was good about cities, what went wrong with cities, how could cities be better, etc. If you are hoping to be a city or county planner, then you might be better off studying administration or bureaucratic theory or underwater pencil pushing. No offense to planners or pencil pushers. I honestly think your trade is one that is as underappreciated as that of builders. After all, we don't turn to planners to plan, we use them to check boxes put in place by committees made up mostly of people who hate each other, when they have actually been trained to plan. Most planners probably have wonderful ideas on how things should be, but instead of asking them how things might work best, we ask them if the project before them meets all the applicable codes, covenants, and restrictions of the General Plan which was put in place by the current (as well as the previous) administration, and whether the council and or representatives present should vote for or against the proposed development based on the proposed plan and budget put forth by the developers present.

I could ride this soap box all the way to the end of the book, but this isn't a book about planning, so I will spare you. Next chapter.

CHAPTER 4

"You never change things by fighting the existing reality. To change something, build a new model that makes the existing model obsolete." — Buckminster Fuller

In the early 2000s while I was attending San Diego Mesa College and UC San Diego, I would take the bus just about everywhere. The public transportation situation in San Diego at the time sucked. It would take me around forty-five minutes to go from my house in Pacific Beach to downtown, and that was after waiting up to thirty minutes between busses. A car ride to downtown was about ten minutes. I'd be surprised to learn that it has changed. However, despite my bitching about the horrible inconvenience of riding the bus, I actually loved it. To me, it was a chance to watch the people who lived around me but I never actually interacted with. Poor people, immigrants, homeless people, young kids, old folks. It was like watching a movie about all the people I knew were around, but I didn't actually know. Occasionally there were times where I was snapped out of my role as voyeur of humanity and compelled to be a character in my own movie. Once a group of savage young boys were blowing spit balls into the hair of an old lady and I just couldn't stand it, so I took my life into my hands and told them to knock it off. They weren't exactly rough kids; in fact, I'm pretty sure they were spoiled rich kids who lived in La Jolla, but there were around five of them, and I was taking at least a small risk by drawing their attention. Luckily they cut it out and I didn't have to fend off any spitballs.

Another time I was riding the bus downtown to meet Pete Perisic, a family friend and soon-to-be mentor who had recently offered me an internship, when the bus driver lost his damn mind. We were cruising down the street doing probably forty miles per hour when I, and most everyone else on the right side of the bus, saw this guy standing on the edge of the sidewalk–right on the curb. For whatever reason the bus was traveling very close to that curb, and all of us on the right side of the bus held our breath. As we passed the guy, missing him by maybe an inch, you could see the guy on the curb gasp and stiffen his body–not moving a muscle.

Some guy from the middle section of the bus yelled at the driver something like, "Hey man, you almost hit that guy!"

To which the bus driver responded something like, "Oh

yeah, why don't you go fuck yourself?"

Which was not received well by the guy from the middle section, and so he said to the bus driver, "I'm going to report you."

The bus driver said, "Oh yeah?"

The guy from the middle said, "Yeah!"

That was the moment when the bus driver completely snapped. He pulled over at the next stop, and as guy from the middle was stepping off the bus (still saying something to the bus driver) the bus driver closed the door on him. He caught him dead center on his chest and back and pinned him in the folding doors. The guy from the middle was pinned by the doors half in and half out of the bus. Then the driver took off and drove to the next bus stop with the guy from the middle yelling and waving his inside and his outside limbs trying to get free. He stopped the bus and opened the door there and dropped the guy on the street. I swear to God this actually happened. The whole bus was just staring in disbelief. The guy from the middle was okay, but not happy. I got off at my stop, walked into Pete's office, and told him the story to which he replied, "You should report that guy." I never did, and I kind of regret that.

...

Petar Perisic was born in Serbia. He came to the United

States when he was a boy and immediately noticed that the cats in America spoke the same language that they spoke in Serbia. This observation only a child could make, and Pete kept something child-like in him into adulthood. Pete was serious about his trade, but never so serious that he wouldn't stop what he was doing to walk downtown to have lunch with an old friend. As my good luck would have it, when Pete was still an actual child, he and his family moved in next door to my aunt in Columbus, OH. Petar grew up in Ohio, went to THE Ohio State University and got a degree in Architecture, and eventually moved to San Diego to open up his own studio. That's basically what I know about Pete's life prior to when I met him in San Diego in 2000.

That first time I met Pete I took the bus downtown, found his building, and walked up the stairs to meet him. "Kelly!" Pete was standing in his office. He was a huge man—not fat, just big, probably six foot three inches—with long brown flowing hair like he belonged on the cover of a romance novel. He stood there smiling at me, emitting the warmth of the sun. He had sharp and powerful facial features, strong brow, prominent nose, and a wolfish smile. Striking. "Want to go to lunch?" he asked. He worked very hard, but he always made time to go to lunch with folks. I think he saw it as part of his job.

Before walking downtown for lunch, Pete gave me a

tour of his studio—the majority of which was dedicated to a gallery space that he and his friend Ken Miracle (what a name, right?) used for art shows which, per tradition, always opened on the first Friday night of the month. I don't recall any art show hanging on the walls that first day I went there. I just remember the super smooth matte-white walls, the wood floor, and the excellent natural light that was coming in from the many large windows that looked down on the East Village below.

The gallery was long and narrow, and most of the walls were laid out at not square angles to one another, which let the light from the windows uniquely illuminate each wall. The space had a special feeling to it even when it was empty. There is something inspiring about freshly painted, pure, matte-white gallery walls. You can't show off a space better than with white paint; it plainly represents the angles, and the millwork—if there is any—and the essence of the space as God intended it. Color in a space is fine, but it hides the true nature of the space itself. I have gotten to the point where I really don't like putting color on walls at all, and I think part of the reason is that I was exposed at a young age to that gallery space that Pete and Ken Miracle had. Over the relatively short time that I was in that studio, I saw some of the most interesting and creative art shows that I have ever seen.

San Diego at the time (I don't think it's changed) was not

a very "progressive" or "artistic" place, and therefore, had a great art scene. I once even heard a guy who was from France, but allegedly had lived all over, describe San Diego as the most oppressive environment he had ever lived in. Maybe that's a bit of a stretch, or maybe not—I don't actually know all the places where that dude lived. Either way, the effect of this "oppression" is that all of the artists in San Diego tended to cling to each other, making for a very tight-knit, cohesive scene. Compare that to a place like San Francisco (which would be my next stop) where everyone is an artist and everywhere is the art district, and you'll find that your art doesn't feel that special.

Art really meant something to Pete, and it was reflected in his architecture—they were one in the same. I never saw him design anything that was just a job. He did fire a client one time because there was a personality conflict; she was famous and her name rhymed with Schmarbara Scmrisand. He never did any work that didn't reflect his brand of creativity. In fact, he never did anything at all that wasn't set in meaning. Even our walks to the Cheese Shop for lunch were lessons on art and design.

I told him once that I wanted to design a bed for myself, and he responded, "Why?"

"Well, I just want to make a really cool bed," I said, not thinking that there was much more to explain about a bed that wasn't already explicit in the word.

"But you need to ask yourself, 'Why this bed? Why any bed? What is a bed?'" I have actually made beds since that conversation, but I don't think I have ever adequately answered that question. To be honest, it still lingers in the back of my mind like an unpaid parking ticket.

Pete one time designed a love seat that looked like a miniature skate park. It was made of bent plywood and steel. The curvilinear shape was meant to allow two people to lounge in it while facing one another. Rather than sitting side by side looking straight ahead (probably at the TV), they would recline while looking adoringly into one another's eyes. This, he thought, was truly a "love" seat. Paul Basil, the furniture maker across the street from his studio, let Pete use his shop to fabricate the seat for an upcoming furniture show. The love seat looked amazing, if not exactly comfy, and most importantly to Pete, his concept was clear. A good design is like a good joke—it needs no explanation, and it makes your mom pee her pants.

I remember sitting in Pete's studio one day and he was critiquing another intern on a building he was designing for an architecture class. The building was to be built in (I want to say) Bangladesh, which has a vibrant culture of textile manufacturing, and was to house the headquarters of some textile firm. The intern had designed a façade for the building of applied, undulating ribbon-like panels, and Pete was giving him the "Why?" and "What for?" and "Why would the building have a textile appliqué?" I remember thinking, 'That's kinda cool, a fabric-like exterior for a fabric company in a fabric country,' but Pete wouldn't have any of it. To him it should be enough that it was simply a building, and slapping some bullshit exterior on it wasn't enough to sell him on the idea. To him the applied fabric-like features were the equivalent of an architectural pun. "Get it? It looks like fabric!" I see now what he was saying. It was a good idea, but you can't just apply some effect to an exterior and call it a day. I think Pete wanted the intern to integrate his idea into the building itself rather than just sticking it to the exterior.

One of my favorite things that I was a part of in Pete's office was when we worked on an installation for an art show that I recall being about reflections on social issues in San Diego. Pete's concept was to create flexible housing for the homeless, but to use construction material in a way that brought attention to the problem of homelessness. The scene he created was straight out of *Escape from New York* or *The Running Man*. Beautiful would not be a word most would use to describe this "scaffolding village" erected three levels high with orange plastic construction netting as walls and wood scaffold planks as floors. I remember at the time trying to add something to the conversation about this idea. I wanted to add my two cents and give Pete some practical ideas about how people could comfortably sleep outdoors, or how we could make attractive homeless "sleeping nooks" at the bases of sky scrapers. Pete listened attentively to my ideas, but I had missed Pete's point of creating these scenes, and it took me until much later in life to finally get it. This project wasn't about solving the homeless problem in San Diego (which was no joke), but instead it was about creating something that would say, "Hey! Look! We have a problem here!" And that it did.

Pete's work was extraordinary. I often find myself doing jobs that I wish I wasn't, but I take them just to pay the bills, and I think most people can relate. Pete never did anything just because, and I would love to know how the hell he pulled that off. It might be because he did some work for a Scmarbara Schmreisand, and then everyone just wanted him to do work for them, but I think it was just a brilliance inside him that could not be denied.

Pete was as dedicated to his craft as anyone could ask from their hero. He lived and breathed architecture and design at large. I'm sure I'm romanticizing a bit here, but what do you expect? He was and is still my hero. One night while working late in his office, Pete had a heart attack and died. He was forty-two years old—eight years younger than his father when he died, also from a heart attack. He was survived by his wife Suzanne and his brother Milan.

The loss of award winning architect Petar Perisic to

architecture and to America's Finest City cannot be over-stated. Pete was doing some of the most interesting, daring, and beautiful work that the architectural community in San Diego had ever seen. Not a single day passes where I don't feel a void from Pete's passing. Literally, every day something comes up where I wish I could ask Pete for his two cents. I could fill volumes with questions that I have for Petar Perisic, and maybe to some degree that is what I'm doing here.

After completing my degree in Urban Studies and Planning I did apply to architecture school, but did not get accepted. I applied to Berkeley and Cal Poly San Luis Obispo. Maybe I shot too high–I did only apply to two schools, and they happen to be two of the toughest programs to get into in California, but what the hell. I thought I was quite the catch. When I didn't get in, I considered bolstering my resume and doing all the things that one does to appeal to admissions offices, but it occurred to me that I could do pretty much everything I wanted to do without an architecture degree if I just started working. I could design houses, and I could build them. The degree is valuable, and I admire all my friends who actually made it happen. Lord knows it isn't an easy task.

While I don't regret skipping architecture school and going straight into my career as a designer and builder, I do wish I had the street cred that an architecture degree/license comes with. Having that degree would give me an edge in marketing myself to the general public; it is a giant neon sign that blinks "Professional!" It also allows you to do things in California that a guy off the street cannot—only an architect can design a three-story house or a four unit apartment building for example (of course there are ways around that). Obviously, the difference between a three-story house and a two-story house is so great and incomprehensible to the average man that only a licensed architect can handle the task. That being facetiously said, an architecture degree by itself a builder does not make. No accreditation organization on earth guarantees the work of its accreditees. It leaves me thinking what's the point? While we're on the subject, can someone explain to me why a notary is a thing? Does a one day class and test make them especially trustworthy compared to the general public? I imagine the court scene where somebody scammed somebody else and a lawyer asking the notary, "Did you see this man sign this document?"

"Yes I did," says the notary.

"Did you realize he was using a fake ID?" asks the attorney.

"No I did not," says the notary.

"Well, I guess I have no further questions," says the attorney.

Is the task of a notary, which best I can tell consists of watching someone sign something, and then writing down notes in a book—not something that any one of us can perform? What's the penalty if the notary makes a mistake? Do they lose their stamp? I guess I should look up the answers to these questions myself, but it just seems so silly to me that we bestow this power of authority on someone after they take a six hour class and test.

Anyways, I know now that licensed in architecture or not, what I do for a living fills a niche that I was put on earth to fill. I believe strongly that what I design now is better informed and more creative than what my same self would be designing at this juncture if I had spent all of my early years architecting rather than building. I do wish I had gone to architecture school, but I also wish I had gone to school for fine art and for law. In the end I did the right thing for who I wanted to be professionally, but I definitely missed out on all that architecture school had to offer. I missed out on the fellowship of other architecture students, the guidance of professors, the fun of having insanely complex and demanding assignments due in way too short a time period, and I respect my licensed architect friends (who are most assuredly not reading this) for going through the rigors of architecture school and jumping through the hoops that the AIA (American Institute of Architecture) puts in place–but in the end I think my training in building actual buildings was more valuable than a degree in architecture would have been. That being said, if any admissions personnel are reading this and want to offer me a scholarship, please get in touch with me.

CHAPTER 5

"A professional is one who does his best work
when he feels the least like working."
—Frank Lloyd Wright

I remember hanging out with a couple of friends after graduating from UCSD and talking about what's next. I told them that I was going to move home and work carpentry for my dad and then figure out the rest from there. They were envious that I had such a clear path forward after school ended. They were both film students and had no idea what they were going to be doing with their lives. It's hard to imagine how I would have looked like someone with a plan at that point in my life. Having your shit together is all relative I guess.

If I were to give my unsolicited advice to a young person (I never would), it would go something like this: You are young and you have plenty of time to make the wrong decision, so just make a decision. It doesn't matter what you do because in the beginning, you are probably going to suck at it, and you will undoubtedly fail a lot, but it is going to teach you something about yourself. Even if what you learn is to never make that specific decision again, that is more valuable than just sitting on your ass waiting for some divine wisdom to hit you upside your head and bring you to the right choice. Don't waste time—just act and start your adventure. The sooner you fail the sooner you recover, and you are bound to fail. And another thing, go get a job in the trades; it will give you something to fall back on and give you callouses on your hands, which are sexy.

I followed through with my promise to my film school friends to move back to Ferndale and work with my dad. My stay at home lasted only six months and I was out of there. I appreciated working with my dad and I did learn from him in that short period of time, but I couldn't really figure out how to be back at home. It's so true what they say: You can never go home. Besides, I was way too charged up with ambition for empire to work under the tutelage of my dad and the hyper-critical reign of my stepmother.

While in Ferndale, a friend of mine introduced me to his friend Chris, who was a handyman/contractor in San Francisco, and he said if I wanted to come down to SF to work with him I was welcome to do so. I asked him how much he would pay me and he offered me $20 per hour, which was double what my dad was paying me so I said, "Hell yes," packed my bag, put my surfboard in my truck, and that was that.

Within a week I think I was working with Chris doing small jobs in San Francisco basically as his partner. We did some decent work around the city and we had a lot of fun. I don't recall ever letting work get in the way of our surfing habit (or our drinking one for that matter). Surfing and contracting go hand-in-hand. To surf every day, when the conditions are perfect, you have to have a flexible schedule. The only people that can pull this off are people who work for themselves or work at night, or people who work for really lax bosses, and possibly housewives (husbands?) and have kids in school, and maybe trust fund kids—but that's it. So, contracting lends itself to surfing. It's a joke in most surf towns that if your contractor isn't on the jobsite, "the surf must be good."

Ocean Beach in San Francisco is one of the best beach breaks in the world and is known for getting really big and staying really good despite the size. There was a period when I was working in San Francisco that I regularly surfed twice a day; I can't even fathom that nowadays, with all the responsibility I have saddled myself with. Boo. Anyways, there I was living the dream: single in the city, surfing every day, making more money than I ever had, and partying just about every night. I would add 'and in the best shape of my life' to that sentence but I was drinking so much beer at the time that my underwear modeling career hadn't exactly taken off. UPDATE: It still hasn't.

Speaking of beer, it is worth mentioning the special relationship of beer and the trades. Being in the trades means that at the end of the day you probably enjoy the taste of a beer more than most. There is nothing like doing manual labor all day long in an attic, under a house, or in a mud hole to make you appreciate the subtle nuance of a Coors Light. Or ten Coors Lights for that matter. Even if you don't like light beer, I guarantee I can give you a job, which by then end of your first day will make you appreciate Coors Light like you never thought possible. There is something about surviving the brutality of a hard week's work that makes a man want to celebrate. You have to celebrate the fact that you did the impossible. I personally don't know what it feels like to be a factory worker on Friday; I'm sure it feels pretty awesome after spending your whole week fitting two meaningless parts together to finally be released on your own recognizance. But Friday in the trades is not only about survival; it is also about victory. The week is done and you have survived the horrible conditions you've put yourself through; you have survived the injuries; you didn't get bitten by a snake or a black widow, and you didn't die from heat exhaustion. You survived, but you also created something, and even if you were demolishing something all week long, you have something to show for it. For that reason, Friday is a celebration. But never forget, sometimes you have to work on Saturday.

Once while building a deck on a Victorian home in San Francisco, Chris and I felt the need to celebrate on Friday the fact that we had survived the week, even though we had promised the client that we would be back to continue work on their deck in the morning. San Francisco has a bit of a reputation for being a sleepy town, but I think that is only in comparison to New York. I found it pretty easy to get off the rails partying in San Francisco, and when you find yourself hanging around with gay guys, it's even easier to get into trouble. Those dudes are crazy. Chris was gay (still is I assume). He and I met up with our friend Shawn and went to a friend's party. After getting sufficiently buzzed at the party, Shawn, Chris, and I decided to step it up a notch and hit up a gay bar called the Stud. I don't know why we did this—Shawn and I are not gay—but I think neither of us wanted to back down.

"You good?"

"I'm good, you?"

"I don't give a shit."

"Me neither."

"Fine."

"Fine."

So off we drove to the Stud. If you go to a gay bar in San

Francisco—the Stud back in the day was no joke—it's good to have a chaperone. Chris told me and Shawn to tell anyone who asked that we were boyfriends. Chris said, "If you tell them you're straight, they'll see you as someone on the fence, and you're dead meat." So we did, and after we dropped our pants for the doorman in order to not pay the cover charge, we entered and proceeded to have about ten drinks. Eventually we left the Stud and Shawn wanted to drive his car home; I wouldn't let him. I actually ended up fighting him in the parking lot for his keys. I won the fight and kept his keys, but in the cab as we were about halfway back to where we lived in the Mission District, Shawn asked me if he could finally have his keys back, and so I gave them to him. As soon as the cab stopped at the next intersection he jumped out of the cab and ran all the way back to his car so he could drive home. What an idiot.

The next day we were hung over like we were fighting the fire at Chernobyl all night, and we *had* to go to work. I couldn't look down. If I had to get something off the ground I would bend at the knees so as not to risk my head spinning completely off of my body. We couldn't get out of working because we had promised our client we would be there. I remember it being a rare hot day in San Francisco, and to add insult to injury we had to lift a bunch of heavy beams into the air to build this massive deck. It was hands down the most miserable day of work I have ever had—and yet one I remember with fondness. Go figure.

Not everything Chris and I built was done well. We were young, learning on the job, and doing most of our work for clients who didn't want to pay for building permits, so there were a few times that we did some things that were a little less than kosher. One example was a bathroom we remodeled where the client wanted us to tile every surface—walls, floor, and ceiling. We did a good job with the tile, but we didn't use a substrate behind the tile, and instead we tiled directly on to the moisture resistant "green board" drywall. This is not the worst thing in the world; in fact it might have been an approved method at one time, but it never sat right with me once I found out that it was not an approved method at the time we did it. For about ten years afterwards, I stayed up at night worrying that with all of the steam and moisture in the bathroom, that the tiles would eventually start peeling off the ceiling and we would be receiving a letter from an attorney. Knock on wood.

CHAPTER 6

"Never order spaghetti in a Chinese restaurant."
—Uncle Jim

Chris and I eventually split up–I think it was because he moved to Jackson Hole, WY to live out his cross-country-cowboy fantasy (the skiing variety), and I needed a new job. My friend and future business partner Matt, who also grew up in Ferndale, was living downstairs from me at the time and had a friend named Dave who said he would hire me. Dave would become a good friend and eventually teach me the glamorous world of production framing.

Production framing is just short for doing a very efficient framing job. At that point I knew how to frame a house from working for my dad, but I didn't know how to do it fast, and I didn't know any of the tricks that Dave and his crew knew like the back of their handsaws. Dave was doing extremely well at the time and had all the accoutrement to go with his success—boat, Harley, fancy truck, and he was building a custom 4,500 square foot house for a wealthy client in Kentfield. When I first started with Dave he had just finished the foundation.

The job paid $25 per hour cash, and came at a time when I was pretty footloose and fancy-free, but I needed work and Dave needed a carpenter. This was not my first job in the trades, but neither was I really what you would call an experienced carpenter. This would end up being one of the best jobs of my life. I came to it when I had zero responsibility in my life, but was making more money than I ever had before. I had the least amount of overhead in my life, and my only desire was to live a simple life—riding my bike almost everywhere and surfing as much as possible. I didn't need the job to pay a mortgage or for child care; I just needed it to get by, and as a bonus it was way more money than I actually needed, so I was quite comfortable.

I believe it is important for young people to have at least one job that they may or may not love, but which they can quit at any time and it won't matter in the least within the whole scheme of things. I feel like people that have never had a mundane and/or meaningless job because they were too focused on making the right decisions to get into the right school so that they can get the right job—a foot in the door for the right career—are missing out. Everyone should have a story of a job where she learned how to simply put her head down and work—not where she learned anything other than *how* to work. And of course, those jobs usually suck, and quitting it will likely be a satisfying experience, but being able to just work is a disappearing trait in kids these days. A shitty job that you do simply for money (and pride) is a rite of passage that will go further towards making a decent person out of you than any amount of formal education.

So, if you are a young person, quit worrying so much about your extracurriculars and go get a job digging a ditch. Digging a ditch, sweeping a floor, stocking shelves, or washing dishes will teach you how to work, and it will teach you how to interact with other humans. Do it while you're young too, because you don't want to be relying on a dishwashing job to put food on your table. These entry level jobs require no training and are the first step to learning a trade. If you start young at learning a trade you can always fall back on that trade if you fall on hard times. Sure, those people who are focused on their careers very early in their lives *might* get lucky and end up better off financially than those who go into the trades, but they might not. Based on about two minutes of internet research I did, I found that mid-career architects tend to average less than journeymen carpenters, but beyond their wage disparity I would argue that the average white collar professional is missing out on what Matthew B. Crawford calls "manual competence" in his must-read (and keep three copies on your bookshelf) book *Shop Class as Soulcraft*. The idea is that by learning a trade you simply learn how things go together, or better yet *that* they go together, and therefore that there is a way to take them apart, fuck with them, and hopefully put them back together correctly before it gets dark.

While I was not the most experienced guy on Dave's crew, I had a strong work ethic, and Dave always treated me like I was a pro. When Larry, Dave's father-in-law, told me he was going to have to show me how to build, Dave reprimanded him and told him to leave me alone. "Kelly is doing fine, you don't need to worry about Kelly." I don't know why Dave had such confidence in me. Maybe he saw that I understood the way things worked or maybe he knew I was the son of a contractor and had building in my blood. Then again, maybe he didn't have a feeling about me one way or another and just wanted to take the opportunity to tell Larry to fuck off. There tends to be a lot of that on jobsites—pissing contests, one-upmanship, shit talking. Either way, it made me feel really good that Dave had my back. To this day I feel very loyal to Dave, and you might be able to trace that loyalty back to the day that he stood up for me; to that one sentence he uttered to Larry.

Working for Dave taught me 90% of what I know about framing a house, but what I value more than the wood-smithing skills I learned was the lesson in blue-collar aesthetics and man-to-man relationships. It takes a tough person to survive on a jobsite around the gruff, sarcastic, rude, and no-nonsense men (mostly) who make up the crews that build the world around you. Or maybe it *makes* a tough person. I don't think most people can handle being dressed down in front of their peers for screwing up, or being told to do something horrible like crawl under a house and clean out the wet fiberglass insulation, "and do it quickly!" Most people who "can't" handle it probably just never have had to, and so are—frankly—soft. I have to deal with softies all the time, and it is a true shock and a blessing when I come across a kid or a laborer who is all in on whatever the job demands. People with gung-ho attitudes like that learned this behavior, and I imagine they did it on a jobsite like the one Dave was running; on which I was lucky enough to have gotten a job.

Conversely, I've only had one desk job in my life; it was in a law office, and it lasted a whole summer. I actually really liked it, and I liked the people in the law office, but I'm pretty sure that 99% of the personalities that exist in the world of the trades would not work out in that office, nor anywhere else in "civilized" society. Before I go too far and make it seem like everyone in the trades is there because they chose the path less traveled, earning their callouses and living out the script of some stoic hero's journey in a modern Western, let me say that there are a lot of people who end up in the trades simply because it is the only place where you might be allowed to work with your shirt off.

We never worked shirtless on Dave's crew, but not because it was prohibited, it was just sort of a bad look. It was unspoken but understood. Plus one of the guys, Dave's brother-in-law, had such a big belly that if he took his shirt off no work would get done because everyone would just stare at him all day long with bewilderment, wondering why he was framing houses and not working in the circus. One day we were driving to the store for lunch and we passed a crew that was working on another house down the street. All of the men working there had their shirts off. They all stopped and stared at us as we drove by, and Dave and I just looked at each other and raised our eyebrows. We didn't say it out loud, but I know we were both thinking the same thing: 'That is one sexy crew.' Personally I like to cover all of my skin with a shirt (and pants too for that matter) just to keep the sun, and most importantly, the sawdust off my body. There is nothing as annoying as sawdust falling down your shirt and sticking to the sweat on your skin.

Most of the social norms that govern a white collar job generally do not exist on a building site. It is okay to swear, spit, and usually even pee outside on a jobsite. I've worked for some very well-educated, very intelligent contractors. I have worked for women, I have worked for some very culturally sensitive hipster dudes, and I've worked for cosmic carpenter/environmentalist hippy types, but no matter how non-stereotypical or socially aware the contractor running the job may be, it never fails that the jobsite is always a place for dirty jokes, tobacco, loud music, yelling, and spitting. And surprisingly, those things are not in the least bit antithetical to peace, love, and harmony in the workplace. On the contrary, making fun of someone's ethnicity or sexual persuasion, yelling, laughing, and singing along to Toto's "Africa" on a jobsite are what keep the rag-tag groups who build most houses sane during a stressful, exhausting, and downright dangerous day of work. I've never seen anyone take offense to all of the horrible epithets that their coworkers hurl at them. I would imagine that this mode of interaction is a unique quality of a building site, or at very least the blue-collar work, and would not serve the same function in most office settings. I would, however, love to have the chance to suggest to someone at Google or Facebook about implementing "Worksite Wednesdays" where you are allowed to work with your shirt off and spit sunflower seeds on the floor while blasting Mexican banda music from your laptop.

While crude and, arguably, macho behavior are common on most worksites, they usually are not the defining characteristic of a specific project. What defines a job is actually the men and women doing the work and, of course, the work itself. With very little exception, I have always worked with people for whom I had immense respect. As is often the case with respect, generally it was not simply given on day one, but was earned by building rapport and through good old hard work. The guys on Dave's crew were typical tradesmen. They were crude but talented; not highly educated but very intelligent; proud like lions, and not likely to talk about themselves.

I have an archetype in mind for carpenters of a stoic-lumberjack-scientist-superhero that I'm not sure is shared by most people. I think most people's stereotype of a carpenter is perhaps a talented guy, but definitely a drunk. Maybe my reverence for builders is old fashioned, but I think it was shared by the general public in the past, and it has just been lost along the way. Even now I look back, and although there were a couple of guys on Dave's jobsite that I never saw eye to eye with, or even liked very much, I have to admit they were good at what they did. They were professionals, in as much as they were experts at their trade, and they behaved like men when manliness was required. We were always real to one another, and we respected each other; as long as your definition of respect includes being able to call somebody a pussy from time to time.

There are a number of reasons for the public's lack of reverence for builders, and I will try to shed some light in this region. For now let's just say that the trades have become a place where you can have a good paying job with very little education, and so a lot of guys end up there. We don't value the trades, yet we need them. Most homeowners see guys that are dressed in clothes that are meant to be ruined on a daily basis, driving a truck that has been beat to hell from work, and who are not well educated, and they categorize these guys as simple (or worse)—even though they are executing a complex skill that takes years to master, and one which the homeowners themselves cannot perform (although most think they can). More on that later too.

Framing that house in Kentfield gave me my first inkling that there was a gap in our collective consciousness between the perception of a builder and the reality. The unique and independent-minded dudes who made up that crew looked—from the outside (at best)—like guys who liked to drink to excess and only showed up to work to support their alcohol habit. And in all fairness, that's not too far off the mark, but what gets lost is that they are drunken masters. In the style of Jackie Chan, they are performing an art that looks a little crazy from the outside looking in, but in reality takes a lifetime to master.

CHAPTER 7

"Don't go around saying the world owes you a living. The world owes you nothing. It was here first."—Mark Twain

(actually Robert J. Burdette was the first to write a version of this quote in 1883, but why let the truth get in the way of a good story?)

I used to ride my bike from the Mission District in San Francisco to Dave's job in Kentfield. One morning as I climbed the last hill before downtown Kentfield, the cold morning fog cooled my face and I remembered that Mark Twain quote, "The coldest winter I ever spent was a summer in San Francisco." So true. Not really true, but at the risk of repeating myself, I am not one to let the truth get in the way of a good story. Anyways, my yellow 1980s era 10-speed actually had ten speeds, but out of pride I only ever used one. The hills around the Bay Area are no joke, and so I was working pretty hard in my ascent. But soon I was at the top and the potential energy I had been storing was released and I began my break-neck descent.

Just as I came over the crest of the hill and the refreshing foggy mist went from friend to foe, I was passed by a beautiful black BMW. I have a thing for BMWs, and was compelled to chase it down the hill. If the street is smooth and the road is windy enough a car and a bike can be pretty fairly matched in a downhill race. The average driver cannot out-corner a bike in extremely tight turns, and the steepness of the hill is all the power the bike needs. This morning the conditions were just such, and I kept up with the BMW all the way down to the bottom of the hill, at times riding so close that I thought I could reach out and touch the car. I think my enjoyment of the moment was shared by the driver as well.

At 7:15 a.m. I rolled up on my teal-green '97 Ford Ranger—parked there since the day before when I left my truck and rode my bike home—and I threw my bike in the back. The twenty-three mile ride gave me the feeling that I had gotten the jump on everyone. Every morning that I woke up early to make that ride, I felt like I was up before the whole world. It also felt like I was doing something besides working, like I had other things going on in my life and was only working because I chose to spend my time that way, not because I *had* to. Of course, I did have to go to work because I was accustomed to paying my rent, but I was only twenty-four at the time, and no twenty-four-year-old really has to do anything.

Trucks will undoubtedly become a recurring theme in

this book. A truck at its core is a big expensive (sometimes ridiculously expensive) tool—arguably the most important tool in a builder's tool kit. The truck carries other tools, materials, and workers to and from a jobsite, and it is hard to imagine doing any significant project without at least a small truck. Yet, it happens all the time.

My buddy Matt and I coined a term for guys that do work without a truck: the trunk-slammer. A "trunk-slammer," a.k.a. "hack," is easily identified in the wild by the vehicle they are driving. It is certainly not a truck, but a car or a hatchback. This person will be very adept at packing tools and materials into their hatchback, and is never opposed to strapping plywood to their roof or running longer material out of the passenger window. No matter how organized and well maintained the hatchback they are driving, there is virtually no way for the guy driving it to have any modicum of self-respect, nor can he anticipate any respect from anyone working at the lumber yard, supply house, or (God forbid) steel fabricator.

Matt and I used to spend hours coming up with make-believe headlines for articles and imagery for covers of our imaginary magazine, *Trunk-Slammers Quarterly*. This publication would be designed with the absolute hack in mind. We would joke about how to use inexpensive MDF (medium density fiberboard, a material that is only slightly more water resistant than cardboard) on the exterior of a building (sadly, I've seen it), or about how to skip town after receiving a deposit, or how to "outsmart" a building inspector. All of the topics in this would-be journal are, sadly, a common occurrence.

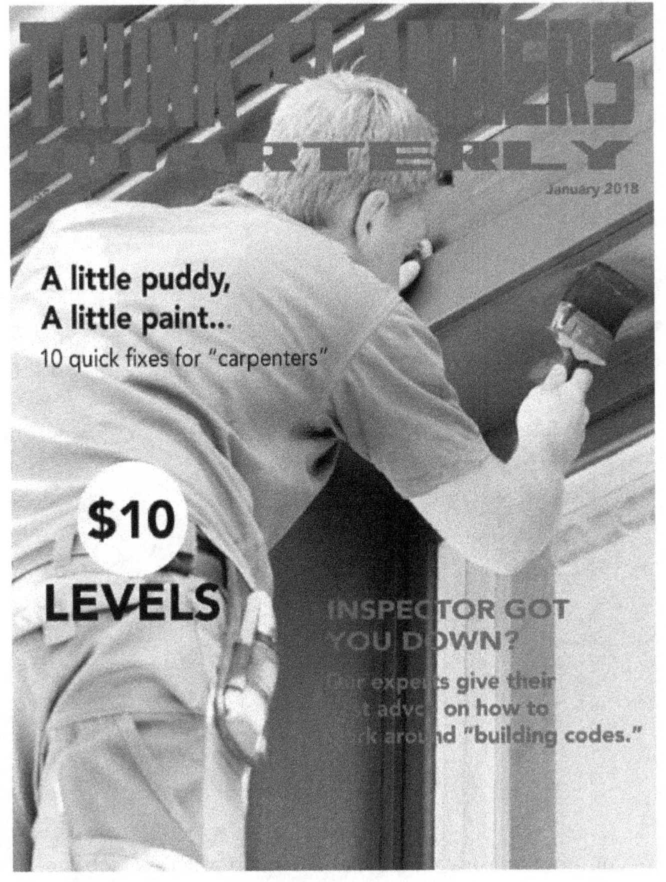
January 2018
A little puddy,
A little paint...
10 quick fixes for "carpenters"
$10
LEVELS
INSPECTOR GOT
YOU DOWN?
Our experts give their
best advice on how to
work around "building codes."

...

The impulse to use a car and not a truck to perform a job is understandable. Like I said before, the truck is an expensive tool. Your first truck, even a cheap beater of a truck, will likely be the most expensive tool you have ever bought. And you probably already have a car. So logic follows...But let me stop you right there. If you are a carpenter and reading this, thinking, 'Hey, what's so wrong with crown molding sticking out the passenger window of my Ford Focus,' here are three really good reasons to sell your car and buy a truck.

Appearances. Nobody wants to see the contractor (licensed or otherwise) pull up to their house in a Chevy Bolt. Their first thought on your first day when they see you parking in front of their house is going to be, "Oh God, what have I done?"

Commitment. I believe commitments are good for people. Make a goddamn commitment. Are you doing this for a living? If you are, then buy a beat up 1997 Ford Ranger for $2,000. If you are not, then get on with your life and go do something else. Get a job working for a guy with a truck.

The opposite sex. You don't want to explain what you do for a living and why you don't have a truck. Everyone knows you should have a truck. Just do it to save yourself the embarrassment of having to justify to your chick why you are storing paint and hand tools in the trunk of your Nissan Stanza. No one finds a dirty construction worker climbing out of a car sexy; stepping down from a truck is what they want to see.

The truck is indeed an essential tool, but it is more than that. The pickup truck is an extension of one's personality. Your truck says something about you the same way your clothes do. It might not be as obvious as that sounds, but conclusions can be drawn from what one drives. If your truck is a total piece of shit, and you take zero care of it, don't wash it, don't fix broken things, then you are making a statement like it or not. Conversely, if your truck is immaculate and has a twenty-one inch lift kit, huge tires, and flawless paint job with all sorts of shiny bullshit accessories attached to it, and you need a step ladder to get your tools out of the back, you are also making a statement.

I drive a white 2002 Ford 150 single cab with lumber racks. My truck doesn't have a name, but if it did it would be something like Steve—just a normal everyday name for a normal run-of-the-mill truck. What my truck says about me is "nothing to see here." I don't put much effort or money into my truck, but I do just enough to keep it in working order. I basically treat my truck like any other tool; if it breaks I fix it, but that is about it.

I had my dog Grace with me at work one day, and when the painter showed up in his lowered, black, super clean Chevy pickup she got excited to see him for some stupid reason—she had never seen him before in her life and couldn't have cared less about anyone else who had already pulled up to the jobsite. Grace ran up to his truck like he was her long lost pal. I don't know why that guy in that truck was the one that made her lose all self-control, but she did and she ran up to his open window, jumped up with both front paws on the side, and slid down the door scratching the paint all the way down.

'With all the beater pickup trucks on this job,' I thought, 'you had to scratch the shit out of the one that was in meticulous condition.'

The painter looked like he was going to cry. Luckily I knew a guy at an auto body shop and he was able to buff the scratches out of the door for no charge. That was the last time Grace came to work with me. UPDATE: I think I am going to take Grace to work with me today. She's getting old, and it's just too sad to imagine her laying on the floor all day with nobody home. Let's hope the roofer didn't just get a new truck.

CHAPTER 8

"I like it when a flower or a little tuft of grass grows through a crack in the concrete. It's so fuckin' heroic." —George Carlin

Eating lunch one day on Dave's job in Kentfield, we began exchanging war stories (which inevitably turn into injury stories, but more on that later). The art of storytelling gets honed on a building site by way of intense practice and punishment. If a story falls flat or is not told well or is just not a good story, one's hammer-swinging coworkers will not be likely to show any mercy. The first and most important rule of storytelling on a jobsite is: Lips Moving, Hands Moving. I learned at a young age that it was important to work and talk at the same time. The brain is able to do spatial reasoning and cognitive activity at the same time, which is why there is usually no problem with music playing on a jobsite, but why music can be distracting if one is writing a bestselling book.

Anyways, we were eating lunch and we were talking about hand nailing (using a hammer), and my buddy Sam brought up a story about a roofing job that he was running for a big roofing contractor that I will try and recreate now:

"So none of my guys showed up that day and we had bundles of shingles on the roof ready to be nailed off, and I had no help. I knew I'd actually be up on the roof that day nailing off shingles, and I called my boss to send me some help." Sam was a supervisor in this story, and so was probably not expected to be doing actual work, but sometimes you got to put your bags on and fill in for losers who didn't show up to work. "He tells me he's got a guy and he'll be there first thing the next day. So I work that whole first day by myself, make whatever minimal progress I can, and the next day I get to the job at seven and *again*, nobody there. I'm thinking what the fuck, this is a nightmare."

A few murmurs come from Sam's lunch-time audience, "Yep, been there."

"So eight o'clock rolls around, still no dude, and I'm just about to call my boss and find out where the fuck this guy is when a truck rolls up. Dude gets out of this old beater of a truck and doesn't say anything. He pulls out a few tools and a cooler from the bed of the truck and I kid you not, opens a Budweiser."

Laughter.

"At this point I'm so pissed off at the situation that I just tell the guy, 'Hey, you do this side, I'll be on the that side', and I just walk off to my side of the house." Sam's annoyance is making everyone chuckle.

"So, I didn't see exactly what tools the guy has brought with him, but I keep waiting to hear his compressor start up, and it never does. I look back at where he was sitting–drinking–and he's not there anymore, but still no compressor. Five minutes later I hear bang, bang, bang! And I'm thinking, 'You're fucking kidding me, he's fucking nailing off the goddamn comp shingles by hand!'" Sam's yelling at this point, and the guys are all laughing joyously.

"No fucking way!" someone says in disbelief. Even old-school Larry, who generally is opposed to using a nail gun would concede that for roofing, it is the only way to go.

"Yeah, I've been waiting a day and an hour for this guy to show up, and when he finally does, he starts drinking beer at eight and no fucking nail gun." He continues, "So, I just put my head down and work. Nailing off as many shingles as I can with the only goal just to move ahead on this job and get on with my life. Between every shingle I think I was muttering the most hateful shit about this guy, and my boss. So, after a few hours I get down from my ladder to eat lunch and walk over to dude's side of the house, and I look up and it looks like there has been an army of roofers working on his side. He has nailed off three times what I was able to do, and he did it all by hand—and had downed at least three Buds before lunch!"

We all just fell about the place, laughing hysterically. "Aaaah! That's awesome!" someone yelled in sheer delight, all of us elated by this small victory for the old school.

Of course, the development of the nail gun has made the building industry more efficient, but as the above story illustrates, it doesn't mean that a master like that beer-guzzling roofer would necessarily be better off with a nail gun. I personally believe that nail guns simply eliminate the time that an apprentice (not really a thing anymore)/novice builder needs to get really good at nailing. Any laborer on their first day can learn to nail off T1-11 siding or plywood very quickly with a nail gun, and thus the building industry at large is made more efficient. On a case-by-case basis, though, a nail gun does not necessarily equate to improved efficiency, and can lead to questionable quality. The problem with framing using only a nail gun is that the nail gun only inserts a nail. It does not move the wood. Usually a quality framing job will require a nail gun and a hammer to tighten the wood after it has been pinned by a nail. So if a quality job is being done you hear: bang! bang! from the nail gun and then the framer pulls out his hammer and whack! whack! to tighten the joint. Bang! Bang! Whack! Whack! It might be easier to do it this way, but not necessarily more efficient, and the temptation to just leave the joints loose and not use the hammer for finishing is strong, especially on a job where the cost is the only driving factor. Dave's job we were framing almost exclusively with a hammer and nails. When you only use a hammer and nail you should be able to sink each nail in two or three swings. Whack! whack! whack! and your joint is tight because that is what the hammer does. The only time we used a nail gun was for plywood nailing (only a psycho would try nailing off plywood with a hammer). I would argue that we were just as fast at framing as a crew using a nail gun, and we didn't have to deal with hoses getting in the way, nor did we have to listen to a compressor all day long.

CHAPTER 9

"Don't worry about the horse being blind, just load the wagon."—John Madden

"What's on tap for today, Boss?" I asked as I buckled my tool bags.

"Don't call me that...or you're buying beers at lunch." As you may have already guessed, beer at lunch is not frowned upon in the trades quite like it would be in a lot of jobs. Think of an office in Manhattan in the mid '50s; a glass of scotch now and then for breakfast was not considered unprofessional. Basically jobsites are just like the show *Mad Men*, only without the sexy secretaries, and instead of suits men wear tool bags and sometimes don't wear shirts. I never saw much drinking on the jobsite, but I will attest to the absolute delight that comes from drinking a couple beers at lunch and then tearing a house down with an excavator. If there is ever an adult-centric amusement park, it will be incomplete without a ride where you get to have a few drinks before demolishing an entire house with a giant piece of machinery.

"You're the boss," I said chuckling.

"Don't call me that," Dave said through gritted teeth–pretending to be angry. Boss certainly was not the right term for Dave–he told me what to do, and how to do it; he hired me, he could fire me, he was fifteen years my senior, and he paid me $1,000 cash every Friday (unless I took time off to surf), but the term still didn't quite fit. Boss implies some guy who is insulated from his subordinates by an invisible wall of superiority, who yells down orders from the corner office. In a boss there is an implied hierarchy; one that doesn't allow the boss to relate to the underling, nor can the boss engage in the same work as his lessor associate. Perhaps with the biggest jobs that have layers and layers of management and hundreds of tradesmen on site, there are bosses who wear slacks and don't ever get their hands dirty, but on most custom home jobsites there is no boss in the traditional sense of the word. The superintendent on most big jobs is not just watching everyone else work, he is also doing work; usually something complex or that requires a bit of head scratching. If said superintendent sees a carpenter flashing a window incorrectly, he will take the time to tell her something like, "Hey Edward Scissorhands, you're ruining the waterproofing on that wall. Let me show you how to do that before you get us into a million-dollar lawsuit."

Dave was not a boss, but he ran the job in Kentfield *like* a boss—although technically Dave's job was actually Bruce's job. Dave was *a* general contractor, but he was not *the* general on this job. Bruce was *the* general contractor on this job, and he hired Dave's crew to do the foundation, framing, exterior doors, and windows, and there was the possibility that we would do the trim. The trim work was a rumor that kept coming up over and over. It was like El Dorado: the Lost City of Poplar! I don't really know what the big deal was, but Larry kept mentioning it and saying things like, "Can't wait to get inside. Gonna wear my loafers to work." Never underestimate the allure of slip-on shoes.

As we were standing and talking about what we were doing that day, Bruce the General appeared out of nowhere.

"Didn't hear ya pull up," Dave said to Bruce, who said something no one could quite hear and chuckled softly to himself.

"I parked down the hill a little bit so I could get a walking view of the house," he said while looking deeply into Dave's eyes.

"Hmm, that makes sense," Dave responded with an annoying lack of sarcasm.

"Ah, snake's eye view!" I said, to zero laughter from my peers.

Bruce (The General) Richardson was an old-school builder who was rumored to have built Jerry Garcia's house close by in the Mt. Tamalpais foothills back in the 1980s. Bruce did not believe in cell phones; he might possibly have been the very last cell-phone-hold-out guy. So as soon as there was something on the jobsite that a landline telephone could be nailed to, he would have the phone company drop a line from the street, and he'd install the "job phone." On this day the phone was hanging on a trimmer that framed the opening of one of the windows in the living room.

"Hey Dave, could you have your guys go around and pick up nails at some point today?" Bruce asked. This struck me as sort of a weird thing to ask, and was all the more weird because he asked Dave to ask the three guys who were all standing right there. Most jobsites are not full of soft-spoken or polite men, but Bruce was just that. Bruce asking Dave to ask his guys rather than ask them directly was a subtle and temperate display of jobsite decorum. You actually run into this hierarchy a lot between contractors. I've had it rub some of my clients the wrong way; for example when my plumber refused to work directly with my client but instead insisted that my client call me first and then have me call my plumber. It might come off as being a bit cliquey or stand-offish, but I think it is really just an unspoken rule that guys follow in order to reinforce the relationships that we develop with our associates, which at the end of the day are the linchpin of any operation—general contractor and subcontractor alike. Bruce was essentially saying, "They're your guys, not mine, and I don't want to step on anyone's toes, so will you kindly have your crew do this thing for me."

Everyone chuckled when Bruce asked this. It seemed like a waste of time to most of the guys on Dave's crew, but I kind of liked the idea. Because we were framing by hand, and we dropped nails here and there, hundreds of nails could end up on the floor by then end of a week, and Bruce did not like the idea of sweeping up perfectly good nails and throwing them in the garbage. I agreed.

To the rest of the crew it seemed ridiculous to pay a carpenter to pick up the nails, and that it was better to pay a laborer to do this work. That may have been true, but we didn't really have laborers per say on that job, and more likely than not the guys just felt like going around picking up nails was beneath them. Goddamn carpenter snobs. I have always been a bit of a math geek, and so that day at lunch I did the math out loud for the benefit of my coworkers, "Four guys getting paid an average of, I don't know, thirty-five bucks an hour—that's 140, times...what...fifteen minutes? That's thirty-five bucks. A box of nails is fifty-five bucks. It almost pencils out!" I smiled and raised my eyebrows, waiting for praise that I knew wasn't coming.

"Almost only counts in horseshoes and hand grenades," said Rick, another carpenter and Dave's brother-in-law. "It's still a waste of my time."

"What do you care, Rick? It all pays the same, picking up nails or building a piano," said Dave.

"It's *close* only counts in horseshoes and hand grenades," said Larry.

"That's what I said," said Rick.

"The problem is that these nails are all made from cheap Chinese steel," said Dave. "Back in the day American nails were made from American steel. Not this recycled shit they use in China."

I laughed knowing that Dave was dead serious, but that he had nothing whatsoever in the way of proof of this conspiracy. I said, "And how does that lead to us dropping nails?"

"They bounce," Dave said with a straight face. "The old nails were sharper and they channeled the energy directly into the wood." I couldn't really dispute his logic, nor could I resolve this idea within myself, so I just nodded hoping someone would save us all with a punchline.

"Fucking China," said Larry. "You know they are building the largest army in the world, don't you?" Larry added.

"What?!" I said. This wasn't exactly the punchline I was hoping for. "Where did you get that?" I asked. This was before YouTube, so I don't know how conspiracies like this one were nurtured. I guess back then you would hear it on Rush Limbaugh and then the conspiracy would be passed from jobsite to jobsite, getting enhanced with every telling like a modern-day version of the campfire story.

"It's true," Larry answered as if he had just put the finishing touch on his argument. I hate when people argue stupid points badly: "Yep, it's true." As if you're a barista putting an oak leaf design in my latte and handing it to me in its perfect, finished state of foam bullshit. UPDATE: I'm less skeptical of this conspiracy now. I hate when that happens.

I love Dave. He is a super smart dude with a good heart, and to this day I consider him a friend and someone I owe a debt of gratitude, but he and his family could really come up with some zingers. Most lunches were spent hashing out the compelling conspiracies of the day. I never had any trouble winning any debate that I got into with those guys, but I don't think I ever converted them to my way of thinking. Honestly, I thought they were wrong about just about everything, but that is not to say that I didn't love going to work every day and being around those lunatics.

As crazy as the men on that crew were, they were good and honest people. They were not anything like the all too common fly-by-night contractors who would screw over your grandmother without losing a minute of sleep. Those guys are out there and you should be very cautious when hiring a contractor to avoid them. It's easier said than done, of course, but the single best piece of advice I can give is that you hire someone to whom you have some sort of social connection. Most contractors live and die on their reputation within their community of friends and neighbors, and they don't want to let those people down by letting you down. The opposite is true too: they will be able to hold you accountable if there is a community in common between the two parties.

Here in Sonoma County where building was going crazy even before we lost 5,000 homes in the fires of 2017, we have had a rash of contractors ripping people off by just taking a huge deposit and then skipping town. They are able to do this because there is so much building going on that there just aren't any contractors available. So, most people will hire someone they don't know just because the guy called them back.

A good friend of mine has been waiting for his final inspection on a fire rebuild in Coffey Park for two years because the contractor skipped town and wouldn't call for the final before he left. My buddy could put the permit in his own name and sign off on it himself, but the that would let the contractor off the hook for any liability if anything went wrong down the road. He finally just contacted the building department and told them that he was living in the house and if they didn't want to final his permit, that it was on them and they could come make him move out if they wanted to. It is uncharted territory for the city and homeowners alike.

The owner of the house we were building was named Daniel. He was pretty well off and didn't really have to work—best I could tell. He was a cool enough guy who hung around the jobsite from time to time to chat with the workers, but he mostly spent his time in his garage—which was completed on the site before the house was even begun (a really good idea by the way)—building the brackets that we would later use to "hold up the barge rafters." I put that in ink-quotes because I'm not sure they actually *did* anything structural, but I don't know if Daniel knew that, and why ruin the guy's story, right? So, if you happen to know a guy named Daniel living in a shingled 4,500 square foot home in Kentfield, don't mention that part to him.

One day Daniel was chatting with us about his house, and he told us, "When this project is done I'm going to have a party and invite you guys and everybody who worked on the house over to see the finished product."

"Oh, right on," I said, "that'd be great. I can't wait to see this place all completed."

"Thanks Daniel, that'll be great," Dave said, almost too politely. Something didn't quite fit about how he responded to Daniel's invite, so I asked him about it a little later.

"That's cool that Daniel is going to have us over for a party when the house is all finished," I said, leading Dave.

"Don't hold your breath," he responded.

Turns out Dave was right. To this day I have never been to a party for the completion of a building project. I have been invited to dozens of parties six months or a year before they actually took place, but never have I been to or heard of anyone else going to the fabled Project Completion Party. In fact, it is pretty much an inside joke at this point. Then again, maybe it's just me and my grating personality that gets me uninvited to the Project Completion Parties that other contractors are actually going to, and they just don't tell me about them in order to keep from hurting my feelings. Dave didn't seem too optimistic about the party actually materializing either.

A likely factor in not being invited to hang out with one's client after completing a project is marriage fatigue. When people are looking for a contractor they are not looking for someone they jive with on a relationship level. They don't look for someone they are attracted to, or who makes them laugh, or is a good dancer. But I think they should. Typically, when looking for a contractor, a client will look for the best price, the most professional looking truck/equipment, well-written contract, and also the best price. Imagine if you looked for a spouse that way. Ignore any chemistry between you and the potential mate, don't listen to your heart, but instead base your decision on the bottom line. What is this, the nineteenth century? I guess a lot of people still pick mates that way, but then again as Americans we don't really have the best track record in that department. Anyways, the relationship one enters into with a builder is just that: it is a relationship. After six or twelve months (or longer) in a relationship, a breakup can be brewing, and the last thing you are thinking about is inviting that person to a fun party with your friends and family.

The most crucial skill, according to me, that contractors need for success in business is relationship skills: How to Be in a Long-Term Relationship With Another Person 101. This doesn't really get taught on a jobsite, and since the jobsite is where 99% of general contractors learn everything they know about contracting, it probably shouldn't be all that surprising that we don't get invited to any parties. In defense of contractors, though, I have to say that most clients are not trained in this area either (like I said before, Americans don't have the best track record), and as always, it takes two to tango. Couple with that the fact that most guys are on a jobsite because they can't really hold a job anywhere else and you are not exactly creating a recipe for interpersonal bliss.

While we're on the subject, the second most crucial skill to success in contracting is getting a law degree. Most contractors are artists, technicians, skilled tradesmen, men's men with little to no use for such flimsy cultural constructs as etiquette, psychology, grammar, or (ironically) even contracts.

The people who get into contracting are not in it for the money, and they definitely are not in it to learn legalese. For most contractors a handshake would be the preferred way of doing business; unfortunately, especially in California, a builder is forced to be a contractor, and a contractor is forced to be an armchair lawyer. Contracts in California are an art in themselves, chock-full of CYA (cover your ass) policies, and loophole-blockers. A construction lawsuit is a sort of rite of passage for California contractors. It says something about the character of builders that they risk their lives regularly—suffering injury and exhaustion on a daily basis—and yet will consistently tell you that regulations set forth by the state and the state licensing board as the worst part of their job. I honestly believe that a lawyer who decides to become a contractor will always do very well. You can always hire skilled workers, but you can't realistically have a full-time lawyer on staff.

I remember talking with Dave and the guys after work one day over a beer (or two or three) about building, and they informed me that one should never, under any circumstances, do work for a lawyer. "Nope. Never. Never ever have an attorney as a client. They will find a way to screw you; it is just in their nature," said Dave.

"Yep, they can't help it," agreed Larry, "they actually have competitions between themselves right out of law school to see who can get away with the most free shit."

"Bloodsucking assholes," added another guy. It was unanimous: no lawyers. I've since had clients who were lawyers and I've never had a problem, but don't think I wasn't nervous when I found out what they did for a living. That one has always stuck with me. Even the most non-threatening areas of law make me really nervous. I recently had a client who was an attorney in estate planning and that was enough to keep me from sleeping.

CHAPTER 10

"It's always funny until someone gets hurt. Then it's just hilarious."—Bill Hicks

I've had friends who worked in offices tell me I'm lucky that I have a job where I get exercise while I'm working. The truth is that it is not really that much exercise. Yes, I walk around, and I do get to carry some heavy shit from time to time, but the actual amount of exercise is something around the level of a beer league softball game–albeit a dangerous beer league, where you might come home from your game missing a finger because the game is played with circular saws instead of bats, and at every base you have to do a geometry problem. Then at the end of the game, someone from the stands who hates softball gets to come down to the dugout and critique your uniforms, your game, and your game plan, to which you respond by giving him your card and telling him you hope to hear from him soon.

There are definitely times where you get your heart rate up. There are a lot of times in building where superhuman strength has to kick in, in order to keep a wall from falling on someone. Or there are times when you need to lift a beam into place while you are perched precariously atop a ladder, and only your buddies running over with their ladders saves you from dropping it. Before I get too carried away with how dangerous every day is, let me also say that I never miss an opportunity to challenge somebody to a wheelbarrow race. Not the kind where you hold another dude's legs (I never get any takers for that kind of wheelbarrow race), but actually filling up and running with a heavy wheelbarrow from pile A to pile B, preferably up or down a hill with a few obstacles for added challenge. A good competition like that is great for morale on a job. While the job itself might not be the best exercise, it certainly does help to be in good shape in the trades. You never know when you are going to have to jump off a roof or do something heroic in order to save someone or something from total disaster.

One such close call happened while working for Dave on Daniel's house in Kentfield. I was nailing off the roof sheeting (plywood) one fine afternoon, and I stepped on a little bit of chalk dust. The roof I was on was a fairly steep 7:12 ("seven in twelve") roof—that is, its slope was seven inches of rise over twelve inches of run, and it was the second story, which meant it was around nineteen feet from the edge of the roof to the ground. Seven in twelve is about the limit of what a person in normal footwear can walk on without slipping, but the microscopic ball bearings that constitute the chalk dust from my string line reduced what little friction there was between my shoes and the plywood, and I began to slide. I looked down to the fast-approaching edge of the roof and quickly started weighing my options. The house was near a fairly steep hill, and in an instant the thought came to me that, 'I'm clearly heading for the edge of this roof, and I don't want to be a guy who died falling off a roof, so I'm going to jump for that hillside.' Even though I was nineteen feet off the ground at the base of the house, the hillside rose up fairly steeply, so I knew that the further out I jumped the less distance vertically I would have to fall. As I slid down the roof and got closer and closer to the edge, I was steadily losing runway for my ill-fated takeoff, and I knew that the sooner I committed to my plan the more speed I would be able to generate, and thus the further out I would be able to jump. I was just about to turn and run down the remaining bit of roof when my fingernails, which had been scraping all the way down the plywood, caught one of the tiny little H-clips (about the thickness of a dime) and was just enough disruption to stop my slide and restore my shoes to their normal state of friction against the roof.

Needless to say I was very careful not to step in any more chalk dust while I finished nailing off the rest of the roof. I'm pretty sure it became law around that time that carpenters were required to wear fall protection at that height, but it is still somewhat rare to see guys using it on jobsites.

Telling stories like that one on a jobsite will always set into motion the notorious injury-story cycle of one-upmanship. Most injury stories start the same way: "Oh yeah? That's nothing! One time..." Dave once was telling me one day that he was on a jobsite when he was a kid (maybe he was nineteen) and a he saw a guy fall off a roof and die. He saw another guy lose an eye from just missing a nail with his hammer causing the 16-penny nail to fly back at the guy and stick straight into his eyeball. On that same job Dave was telling us all about the time he was nailing off plywood sheathing on the side of a really tall chimney (chimneys built in seismically active areas today are now usually framed with wood and plywood and then covered in rock or brick to look like the widow-makers of yesteryear). He was on the tippy top of an extension ladder—probably twenty-five feet up to the rung he was standing on, and was nailing the plywood sheathing to the wood framing. The width of the chimney was such that stretching out he could just reach each side of the plywood without having to move the ladder. This feat of athleticism becomes harder as you get nearer the top because as the ladder, and therefore your body, gets closer to the wall, you are forced to straighten up rather than being able to lean into the building.

Dave said he was just getting to the very last couple of nails and reaching out as far as he could with his right hand on the nail gun and the other on the wall for what little grip he could generate when the ladder started to slide in the opposite direction. Out of pure reflex he swung his right hand, still holding the nail gun, back to the center, but never let go of the trigger, and as his right hand (and nail gun) met his left hand (flat against the wall) he nailed it to the wall right through the fleshy web of skin that is between your thumb and forefinger.

Dave said, "I was actually lucky because with my hand nailed to the wall it gave me enough grip to stop my slide, and I could pull the ladder back beneath me with my feet. I grabbed my catspaw and pulled the nail out. I was done nailing the plywood so I just climbed down the ladder." I don't remember if Dave said he went to the hospital, but I kind of doubt it. There is definitely a code of toughness on a jobsite that says, in short, "Don't be a pussy." Apparently going to the hospital for anything less than a life threatening injury is being a pussy. I find toughness to be an admirable (albeit waning) quality in a person, but you have to realize that there is a difference between toughness and plain old stubbornness. And ultimately, there is no bonus check at the end of your career for being tough but crippled.

One of the worst injuries I ever witnessed was sustained by a woman for whom I was building a deck. She was helping me do the shade structure that sat above the deck and installing some wood blocking in between the rafters. One of the blocks she was installing was a little too big, and instead of climbing down off the framing and cutting a cunt-hair off the block (the book would be incomplete without at least one reference to the universal measurement for all things tiny, slim, slight, or short) she was slamming it into place with her hammer. She was a moderately experienced carpenter, and more or less knew what she was doing, and it was *her* deck so I didn't really feel it was my place to tell her that she was being lazy and should just climb down and cut the block smaller. I also think there might have been something else on her mind because she was really letting that block have it. Anyways, she was sitting up on the rafters wailing away on that poor block when wham! she connected with her finger. Immediately, yet relatively calmly, she said, "Oh fuck. It's broken. It's broken."

"It's not broken," I said, not actually knowing but trying to keep her calm.

"It's broken," she said, and then showed it to me. I could see that finger had one extra joint and it was bending the opposite way of the other joints. It was very clearly broken.

"Okay, it's broken," I conceded. She was really calm and still. I've always heard that women are better at handling pain than men, and judging by her reaction in that moment I'd say that holds water. She asked me to help her down from the rafters, and when I lifted her up to set her down on the deck I could feel her trembling ever so slightly.

I personally have had my share of close calls. None as close as the time I nearly killed myself in a propane explosion. Let me say this first as a public service announcement: if you ever encounter a brand new propane tank, the gas inside might not be odorized. For whatever stupid reason, the odor, mercaptain, dissipates in a new tank to the point that the whole volume of the tank is rendered odorless, and thereby extremely dangerous. This was the case in an underground tank that I had installed in a client's home I was rebuilding after the Camp Fire of 2017. As we neared completion of the build, my clients were starting to stay weekends at the house before they had their occupancy permit, and so one Sunday they called me up to see if I could diagnose why the water heater wasn't working. It would work, then it wouldn't. So, being the helpful guy that I am, I drove over to their house in my flip flops and traditional Sunday leisure wear to see if I could help.

The error code on the water heater said it was not getting gas. This is not uncommon in a new construction situation, especially if you have a long distance of pipe and/or large diameter pipes, both of which contribute to large volumes of air before the propane in the tank displaces the air through normal use. The normal course of action in this situation is to crack open the propane line at the appliance and let the air out of the line. Usually you can tell that this has happened because the pitch of the gas whistling out of the line changes when the gas goes from normal air to propane. In my case there was no pitch change, and we never smelled any gas. There was no pitch change because there was gas already in the line from days of running the water heater trying to get it to work consistently. I read the error code as "no gas," but the problem actually was not enough gas pressure. The error code was not that specific, and because the gas was not odorized I took it on faith that there was no gas in the line, which again, was backed up by the error code on the water heater.

So, long story short, after being stumped by the situation I stopped what I was doing and put the gas line back together and plugged the water heater back in. As the prongs of the heater touched the outlet, the connection made a small arc and ignited the room that was at this point pretty full of gas. The whole room exploded, cracking the drywall and blowing tile off the kitchen backsplash which was on the opposite side of wall, and blowing the screen out of the open window. The fireball burned me on about 20% of my body—everything that was exposed got second-degree burns, and left me in what would turn out to be the most painful ten days of my life. I still can't even watch people getting burned up in action movies without getting chills down my back.

Hopefully that experience yields some benefit to my friends, colleagues, and you dear readers—don't fuck around with propane. If you think there is even a slight chance of gas being in the room with you, don't make any damn sparks!

In a list from Bankrate's article "*10 of the most dangerous jobs in the US,*" (May 9, 2016) two of the ten are in the building trades: roofers and structural steel installers. And, according to *The Washington Post*, five out of the top twenty most dangerous jobs are construction jobs: roofers, construction laborers, painters, and electricians ("Charted: The 20 deadliest jobs in America," January 28, 2015). You don't necessarily need to be a tough guy to work in construction, but you do need to deal with the reality that you are more likely to die at work than the average bear. You also need to deal with daily pain. I don't think you could find a tradesperson who didn't display a consistent array of nicks and scratches on their hands. Maybe painters? But even painters get a fair share of cuts while they are prepping buildings for paint. If you've ever painted your own house and spent the time to do it right by prepping the surfaces you know that painting should actually be called scraping and sanding. Our hands are incredibly useful tools, but even over two hundred thousand years of human evolution they are still covered in nothing but skin. Some guys wear gloves, but most don't. As I am typing this I am looking down at no less than four cuts, one blood blister, and cuticles that are simply atrocious, and I can't really remember how any of the blemishes got there.

CHAPTER 11

> "Until then it had been my intention to visit his country as a friend, to see and talk with him, and hold much peaceful intercourse with him."
> —Hernán Cortés

Not long after we finished working on Daniel's house (we never did get hired for the trim portion of that job), I got an opportunity to move to Mexico and volunteer at an orphanage in the city of Colima, in the state of Colima. Uncle Jim and Aunt Penny had been going down there for thirty years at that point, and I had always heard stories about the "Casa," as they referred to it.

I had a friend from high school named Carrie who was planning on going with me, but she backed out at the last minute. I am so grateful that she did because I think if she hadn't, I would not have had the same experience of immersion into a foreign culture that I did. I didn't know it at the time, but by having no one with whom to speak English or reminisce about all things USA, I was going to get a life-changing educational and cultural experience.

I arrived at Casa Hogar de San Jose in Colima on the same day as a letter my aunt had written to the director of the orphanage. The letter was intended to tell the director of the Casa that I would be coming down to volunteer. Back then mail was ridiculously slow in Mexico, and email was still catching on for people over fifty (Mexican and American alike). So, I sat in the office of the director of the orphanage, whose name was Lupita, while she read the letter. She occasionally lifted her eyes to mine and smiled. I spoke only the remedial basics of Spanish at the time—the result of three years of C-level effort in high school Spanish. Lupita spoke even less English, and the same was true for the rest of the people living and working at the Casa Hogar.

While Lupita read, I sat in silence and took in the setting around me. The smell of burning yard waste—a constant in most of Mexico—hung in the air, and the mildly oppressive heat of the morning reminded me that I was a stranger in a strange land. Colima is consistently one of the warmest places in Mexico, so much so that they say when people from Colima die and go to hell they bring blankets. The concrete buildings of the orphanage were not insulated, nor did all of the rooms even have glass in the windows, but rather just metal bars to keep people and animals out. Everywhere on the compound was essentially the same temperature all the time, with the exception of the kitchen which seemed to be a couple degrees cooler all the time probably due to its location below and behind the larger building that housed some of the huérfanos (orphans).

Lupita finished reading the letter, set it on the desk, and looked up at me with a smile and said, "Pues, bienvenidos."

I think I probably said, "Hola." My Spanish was seriously lacking at that point, but thanks to the fact that I was traveling alone, and no one else in the orphanage spoke English, that problem quickly began to be remedied. In about three weeks I was speaking Spanish—all that high school vocabulary and grammar must have worked its way into a dark corner of my brain and wedged itself in there only to finally be dislodged when my life depended on it. Upon returning from Mexico, I decided I needed to write a letter to the students of my high school Spanish teacher, Mrs. Potepan. I told them that even if you are a C student, you are learning something that one day could surprise you and give you access to another culture. Don't worry if you suck at Spanish, just let it wash over you and infect your brain the way it did mine, and one day it might all make sense.

Lupita showed me to a bedroom, where I was to stay until my actual room was prepared, and then she showed me around the grounds of the orphanage, which housed around eighty "niños" between the ages of three and eighteen. In exchange for room and board, I was expected to help with day-to-day maintenance of the buildings, run errands in the Volkswagen bus called "el Combi," and maybe come up with a few projects here and there that would somehow get the orphanage running a little smoother. That last part I might have made up; it may not have actually been an explicit request to try and make the orphanage run smoother. After all, the Casa was there before me and would live on after me, but what's a gringo supposed to do? It was not uncommon for gringos like myself to come to the Casa Hogar with grand ideas for improving the place. Most of said ideas were not practical for the Casa to maintain, but were nonetheless implemented to greater or lesser degrees of long term success. I definitely fell into the category of the stereotypical gringo looking to make improvements, although that faded with time as I realized that the Casa (much like Mexico at large) was pretty content with the status quo.

As one of two people on the compound with a driver's license, I was by default the main chauffer to anyone who needed anything from town. Technically I wasn't supposed to take people into town if it wasn't directly related to the needs of the Casa, but not knowing Spanish very well meant not really knowing who was conducting Casa business or personal business, or God knows what other kind of business.

I eventually learned how to tell the difference, but it took a few weeks to learn who was who, and even then it was hard to say no, particularly when the Combi had a giant opening on the side where the sliding door was supposed to be.

The Combi was wide open all of the time, so people could just jump in through the side of the bus as I was leaving the grounds. Sometimes I would leave the Casa with ten people in the Combi, each with their own agenda. Ultimately I developed a technique for leaving the Casa that was less likely to engender stowaways: I would quietly open the gate, push the Combi down the slight incline of the driveway, and then just as I reached the open gate I would pop the clutch, hit the gas, and tear out of the Casa grounds like I stole something. This worked pretty well, but there were many days where I would be tearing out of the Casa grounds and kids and adults alike would chase after me yelling, "Kelee, Kelee" and some would dive through the opening in the side of the moving bus. It actually got to the point where we had to put a door on the Combi because it was just plain dangerous, even by Mexican standards.

I absolutely loved that old Volkswagen. When it broke down, I fixed it, usually from parts of other rotting Volkswagens on the property. I swapped out the engine in a day and the transmission in another, which is a testament to the simplicity and beauty of old Volkswagens much more than it is to my skills as a mechanic. We put a door on it, as I mentioned, but that fix was not very satisfying because there is nothing like driving around Mexico with no door and having people laughing and yelling your name as you drive by.

The guy who helped me with just about everything I did at the orphanage was named Pancho. Pancho looked like the stereotypical round Mexican that you see in Speedy Gonzales cartoons napping in a hammock. He spoke with a raspy mumble that I never fully learned to decipher, and being the most laid-back person on earth, he was endlessly amused by my impatient approach to getting things done around the Casa. We made quite the team. Like me, Pancho knew a little about a lot, and unlike me, he knew Spanish and he seemed to know each of the three hundred thousand people living in Colima.

Most of the time the fixes that I implemented on the cars and trucks at the Casa were Band-Aids at best. It was always hard to find parts for things in Mexico; either I knew what part I needed but didn't know what to call it, or I knew what to call it and yet the store didn't know what I was talking about, or I knew it and the parts store knew it, but they just didn't have it. Fortunately, I usually had Pancho with me to help in the communication department, although I think Pancho always preferred to hear me torture the Spanish language for as long as possible before giving me the right words to say.

Pancho always put humor ahead of efficiency, which I respected, but it was not simply because he had an epic sense of humor. Efficiency in Mexico is a foreign concept. It takes a mighty effort to get anything done in Mexico, and even then you have to know the right people, and even then it helps to pay a bribe. Bureaucratic red tape and corruption within the government is innate in Mexico, and you can see it in something as simple as getting a car registered. In the US, the thought of bribing a government official in order to get your car registered is unthinkable because the consequences of going to jail far outweigh the benefits of not standing in line at the DMV for an hour. But at the Casa our thought process usually started with, "well, obviously we can't just go get this old Volkswagen registered; who do we know and how much would it cost to get fake plates?" Not that we ever did that, but it's a starting point. There is a bit of a fatalistic mentality shared by most Mexicans in this regard. What's the point in being efficient when the system you are inevitably going to come up against is mired in corruption? You can be the most efficient worker in the whole country, but what difference will that make when at the end of the day you have to pay someone to "find" your "lost" paperwork?

The other problem with being a shadetree mechanic in Mexico is siesta. Siesta happens every day approximately between twelve and three (I think–I'm still not sure exactly when it happens), and always coincides with one's need for parts. I could never get used to siesta; don't get me wrong, I think it is a fine idea—taking time at home with your family, eating lunch, napping during the hottest time of the day—I am for all of these things. My problem was that I am not wired for taking breaks. I simply could never remember that siesta was daily occurrence. Every other time I went to a store for a car part or a water heater part or any other part, the store would be closed for siesta. Same time every day, but I couldn't get it through my head. This frustrated me to no end, and I think it made Pancho's day. The flip side to siesta is that most stores stay open until 10:00 p.m., so if you are burning the midnight oil and need a part, you can go get it—this I could sign up for.

On any given day in the Casa Hogar San Jose compound, at least ten of the twenty or so water heaters that serviced the eighty or so kids plus staff would not be working. It was always so hot in Colima that not having hot water was not as big of a deal as it might be in the States, but eventually someone would tell me about it and I'd have to go and fix what was wrong. Every water heater in the Casa, and I would guess 99% of the water heaters in the entire world, operate with thermocouple technology that uses a lit pilot light and a thermostat. I have probably diagnosed over one hundred of these pilot light/ thermocouple setups, and I can say without hesitation that spiders the world over are genetically predisposed to end humanity's ability to heat water. They crawl into the tiny orifices that lead from the pilot light back to the gas source, and they leave a little bit of cobweb that blocks the gas. If you are having trouble getting your pilot light to light, then you can bet that a spider is to blame.

If I wasn't on official Casa business, I would not be getting around using the Combi, so once again I found myself on the bus and loving it. The "camion," as they are called there, was the cheapest and easiest way to do short trips, and it was a great way to experience the locals in their element. The day I boarded my first of many camiones with a six foot surfboard in tow, I'll admit I did feel a bit out of place. I wondered what the locals were saying to each other about the gringo with the surfboard taking up way too much space on an already overcrowded camion—probably something along the lines of, "what the hell is this gringo doing with a surfboard on our already overcrowded camion, and over an hour from the beach?" That's probably all in my head; Mexicans have an impressive tolerance for silly behavior. Anyways, surfboard in tow, I managed to communicate with the indifferent driver as to the fare—eventually just holding out my money and letting him take what I owed. For what it's worth, camion technically means truck, but is also what they call the local busses in Mexico. Go figure. Bus (or autobus) is the word reserved for the much nicer longer-distance bus; the nicest of which rival first class accommodations on most airlines. If you ever need to travel a long distance within Mexico, it is the only way to go.

That day I was bouncing around (literally) in the camion, and marveling at the speed and skill with which the driver was navigating his course. I haven't been to that many countries outside of the Western Hemisphere, but I would imagine that the experience on local busses is the same the world over. Much like my time riding the bus in San Diego, riding the bus in Mexico put me dead center into the lives of so many ordinary, and mostly poor, people. I'm sure everywhere must be the same; if you want to see what average people do for a living, what they buy at the store, what they talk about, where they live, where they shop, then ride the bus. Our driver that day was navigating the road like a rally car driver, but his driving skill was nothing compared to his verbal dexterity. He had the front half of the bus, mostly women, totally engaged in the gossip (chismes) of the day. I couldn't understand what they were talking about, but clearly it was gossip, and he was the instigator calling out people where they deserved it, talking shit to people's faces as they got on the bus and talking behind their backs after they disembarked. The guy had me cracking up, and I couldn't understand a word he said.

I got off the bus in the town of El Paraíso and as the sound of the bus and roaring laughter faded away, I could hear the waves crashing just on the other side of the palapa-roofed buildings. I walked over to the beach and put my stuff down in the shade and marveled at some of the cleanest shoulder-high waves I had ever seen. I thought, 'Is it like this every day here?' The answer is no, but damn near. El Paraíso means paradise, and it was living up to its name.

After a pretty satisfying surf session I laid down under one of the ramadas, which is basically four posts in a square with palm leaves covering the roof, and stared up at the structure I was under. It was as simple a structure as I could imagine. Four posts, four beams connecting the posts, some "rafters" over the beams and palm leaves on top of that. There was also a kitchen built nearby with not much more than a griddle, a burner, and some ice chests. There might have been running water. Next to the kitchen was a super dark-skinned guy in board shorts and flip flops lounging in a hammock–one leg in and one leg on the ground. I deduced that this was his ramada, and his wife and daughter inside cooking the occasional taco, eggs, or quesadilla. The simplicity of the situation was overwhelming. A simple structure twenty yards from perfect waves, a simple kitchen with no actual menu, one hammock, and a family of three surviving on what could only have been a meager income. What glazy-eyed surfer wouldn't give deep consideration to quitting his job and moving to Mexico to take their place?

It made me think, 'Here are three people surviving on very little. They are alive, have clothes, and feed themselves. They presumably have shelter, and although they may not have the best health insurance, and probably don't go on many vacations, they live in paradise. Literally.' There was nothing special about these people; there were hundreds of families just like them up and down the beaches of Mexico. Anyone who wanted to live this lifestyle could do so. And yet there I was, wanting to live that freely, but I knew I couldn't. The pull of my gringo way of life was too strong. The potential energy that I had been storing up would never be overcome laying in a hammock under a ramada with my wife cooking quesadillas for kids day-tripping from Guadalajara. Eventually all of the things that I had been learning and planning and unconsciously preparing myself for would break out, and I would have to destroy that idyllic life.

As I lay there thinking these thoughts and analyzing the construction of the ramada, a guy walked up to me and asked if the baby blue surfboard next to me was mine. I told him it was, and he asked if he could try it out. His name was Germán, and this would be his first ever surf session. Germán was a naturally gifted surfer and we hit it off immediately. Germán and his girlfriend offered to give me a ride back to Colima, and we became good friends. We are still close today.

It didn't take long for me to start planning my future in Colima. Lupita was sanguine about the idea of me taking over the ranch that the orphanage owned and turning it into a working organic farm. I was constantly coming up with schemes to make the place generate income. I had ideas of eco-tourism, philanthro-tourism, fabrication and exportation of Mexican arts and crafts; I had high-end retreat concepts and grand architectural aspirations.

As I said, red tape in Mexico can get out of control, and therefore there is also a robust gray area that exists above, below, and around all of the bureaucracy. You can pull a building permit in Mexico, but hardly anyone does—especially for a residence. There is very little restriction on what you can and can't do with your property, architecturally and otherwise. If you know the right people, and are prepared to grease the right palms, there is nothing you can't eventually build in Mexico. Sometimes I wonder if I had stayed there and pursued design-build in Mexico, if that would have advanced my career further and faster than here in the States.

I guess we'll never know because that didn't happen. As much as I loved (and still love) Mexico, its people, its beaches, its weather—and the list goes on—I was a stranger in a strange land, and I was basically alone. If I could have convinced one friend to come down to Colima and help me with my grand schemes, I'd like to think I could have toughed it out and gotten through the feeling of homesickness, but alas, I couldn't. To add insult to injury, my girlfriend got impatient and broke up with me while I was gone. I can't really blame her after all of my talk about not coming home, but that didn't make it sting any less. After six months my Aunt Penny and Uncle Jim came to visit, and as they prepared to return to California, I couldn't bear the thought of them leaving without me. And just like that, my stay in Colima, all my plans, and my story came to an abrupt end. In two weeks I was back in San Francisco remodeling someone's bathroom.

CHAPTER 12

"It's just a job. Grass grows, birds fly, waves pound the sand. I beat people up."
—Muhammad Ali

Not long after coming back from Mexico, I started working for another Dave. Up until that point I had held four jobs in the trades: a half year with my dad, a half year with my uncle Jim, a year with my gay partner Chris, and a half a year with Dave in Kentfield. I worked for Dave #2 for another year or so, and then decided I was ready to go it alone with my very own design-build company that I named EPIC Design-Build. Looking back I can't believe the audacity I had to think I was ready to work for myself. But I did, and I started designing and building mostly smaller projects after a grand total of maybe three years' experience. I did grow up with a contractor father, so you could say that building was in my blood, and according to the Contractor's State License Board, I had a degree in a building-related field, but still, I don't think I was very well prepared to be out on my own, and it is only by the grace of God that everything more or less worked out in the early years.

I think my experience with Dave #2, a young man only a couple of years my senior, may have made me naively think, 'Well if Dave #2 can do it, why can't I?' What I was missing was how hard it actually is to run your own business, let alone a contracting business. I thought at the time, 'Dave #2 is young; I am young. He knows things; I know things. This will be easy.' While he was successful, it wasn't easy for Dave #2, and I didn't realize how hard it actually would be for me. Which, by the way, is why you should take risks when you're young. Who cares if you fail? As long as you don't physically hurt yourself, you will recover. If you are a young person thinking of starting a business—contracting or otherwise—stop reading this book and go start it. Today. Right this minute. The sooner you get your feet wet, the sooner you will inevitably fail, and the sooner you can pick yourself back up and do it right the second time.

The barrier of entry for the trades is quite low, and to the untrained eye a skilled craftsmen and a total hack can look a lot alike. See: trunk-slammers. Fortunately for me (and my clients), I never bit off more than I could chew and I always charged my clients a fair price for decent work. I certainly was no master builder back then, but building was all I ever wanted to do, and although I may not have known it when I was younger, everything in my life was leading me towards a career in building.

Back then I was learning on the job, and I made mistakes on every one of them. But every mistake I made, I paid out of my own pocket to fix—what my builder friends and I came to call "tuition." If you quote someone a price on a job, it is your responsibility to complete the job for that price—even if you screw it up in the process, even if it costs you money to fix your mistakes. Those costs are the tuition you pay to the school of master building.

Of course not every contractor chooses the path of becoming a master of their trade. I heard once about a sprinkler contractor who ripped off his client by not actually installing any sprinkler pipes in the attic of the building he was hired to "sprinkle." He simply went through the home and stuck the sprinkler heads into the drywall so that it looked like the home had sprinklers, sent for his final invoice and, you guessed it, skipped town. That is one of the worst contractor stories I've ever heard, and I'm pretty sure that guy was risking jail time if he ever got caught. Another word of advice: avoid any contractor whose company is called Fast Eddie's (fill in the blank).

One of my classic tuition moments came before I went to Mexico, when Chris and I were remodeling the house that he was actually living in at the time. The house was owned by his friend Barry, and we were in the process of demolishing the kitchen in order to update it and make it bigger. One of the moves we were making was to take some space from the closet and give it to the kitchen. I began cutting through the studs that framed in the closet because it is easier to remove studs if you cut them in half and then just wiggle them loose from the nails. I was working from the kitchen side of the wall with my Sawzall cutting through the studs. We had removed the lath and plaster from the kitchen side of the wall, but hadn't removed it from the closet side of the wall in an attempt to minimize the dust and overall discomfort for our client Barry, so I couldn't actually see into the closet. I was about a quarter of the way through the wall when Chris said to me, "Did you take Barry's clothes out of the closet?"

"Oh fuck!" and I ran around the corner to look. Sure enough, I had cut three inches into the sleeves of about six shirts.

I believe if you added up all the money that I have paid for mistakes-made-good, it would easily be more than that goddamn architecture degree I never got.

Every little moment and every little story like that one add up to define a career, for better or worse. You have to make good on your mistakes and pay that tuition or you won't progress towards that blood, sweat, and tear soaked diploma. A major turning point in getting my building degree came just before I went to work for Dave #2. I was remodeling a bathroom in a giant building in the city. I had all of the walls open and it was time to shut off the water, so I could cut the old copper plumbing out and solder in all of the new stuff. In a building like this you can't just go out to the street and shut the water off yourself; you have to call the maintenance guy, who in this case was an actual plumber with an actual job other than turning the water on and off.

So, I call for the plumber/maintenance man and he shows up and tells me he is going to turn off the water and asks, "How long do you need to do all the plumbing?"

"Uh...I guess a couple of hours?" I tell him with zero confidence.

"Okay," he says, "I have another job going, so call me when you're done and I'll be back."

"Okay," I gulp. The thing about "sweating" copper pipe, or soldering the joints to the pipe, is that there is a little bit of an art to it. Of course, I learned to sweat pipe from Uncle Jim, and he did a decent job showing me the basics, but like anything tricky it takes practice to get good at it. The most important thing is to keep the connections clean, and the second most important thing is to keep them dry.

So there I was, left alone to solder my pipe and hopefully get it done in one pass. I was initially hoping that the maintenance guy would just be hanging around so that when I was done I could have him turn the water back on in the apartment, and most importantly, if there were any leaks he could turn it back off, and then on, and then off again until I had it all figured out. But that was not the case, and this surly plumber did not strike me as the type of guy who was interested in hanging around while I learned how to properly sweat copper fittings. Nope, this guy expected me to know what the hell I was doing. After about four hours I had all of the copper reconnected, and all the new valves in place. It wasn't pretty–I had solder all over the place and a few charred studs here and there, but it was done, so I called the maintenance guy. He showed up and said, "Okay, I'll go turn on the water."

To which I responded, "Okay, will you be within earshot so I can yell to you in case there is a leak?"

He explained that he wouldn't be close enough to hear me because the valves were was on a completely different floor. He stepped into the bathroom, took one look at my soldering job, paused, and said, "There won't be any leaks."

What? How could he know this? Of course there would be leaks, there were always leaks. Obviously he wasn't looking at the work of a pro here; my soldering had to look sloppy as hell to this grizzled old pipe fitter. Guys like him probably cleaned every joint to be almost completely free of solder except for a very small ring around the joint. His work was probably art. My work looked like a half-melted ice cream cone at every joint. There was something about soldering pipe that I had never figured out (I guess I was only twenty-four, but it seemed like I had been having soldering problems for a lifetime). I *always* had leaks, and if you have ever soldered pipes, you know that once you get leaks it is usually a nightmare to fix them. Water gets into the pipes and prevents you from being able to heat the pipe up enough to bond the copper and solder, and a lot of times you end up having to cut out what you did and redo it. There is always a trickle from a seemingly inexhaustible source that you can never get to stop in those situations. Somehow this gnarly old plumber looked at my globbed-on, overly soldered, and sloppy mess of a plumbing job and stated with full confidence, "Won't be any leaks."

"Okay," I said, "I hope you're right."

He left and went to turn the water back on, and when he returned he looked into the bathroom. "Any leaks?"

"No," I said astonished.

"Told ya," he responded, and then left to go about his day.

I have never had soldering problems since.

...

Because the average white-collar professional does not spend any time looking at the systems hidden in the walls of her office or under the hood of her car, she does not gain insight to the way the physical world actually works, but instead has to take all of the systems around her on faith. She turns on the light switch and light fills the room, and she is never forced to contemplate the system itself. This is becoming bizarrely true even in the computer programming world, where the very programmers on the cutting edge of computer learning don't know exactly how the algorithms they are writing are actually working to give their computers what is fast approaching self-awareness. Check out the article by Will Night called "The Dark Secret at the Heart of AI" (*MIT Technology Review*, April 11, 2017) that describes this in detail.

This ignorance of how our world works is never as frustratingly obvious as when something in your house or your car breaks. Even the present-day architect, who in theory should be well-versed in the various systems that make up a building (i.e., framing system, flashing system, heating, electrical, plumbing systems) would be hard-pressed to diagnose, troubleshoot, or fix any problem with any of those systems. This is not a fault of the architect as I see it, but instead a fault of the values system in place at the institutions that are training architects. Had that architect had a summer job doing electrical with his uncle Leroy, he would undoubtedly have gained some specific understanding of at least some parts of the systems that make up a building. Even if all he has done is worked as a plumber's assistant for a couple of summers, if he's a halfway-aware person he would glean a deeper understanding of the house at large, and also how his trade interfaces with the other trades around him. He would see the systems running through the open carcass of the building, and see the intersections of plumbing and roofing, electrical and framing. He would see the anger of the HVAC guy when the plumber crushed one of his air ducts, and in their argument gain an understanding of why the plumber did what he did, and why the HVAC guy was so pissed off. The architect-to-be would gain a fuller understanding of the built environment just by being in the room with all of these technicians. If he's paying a little bit of attention it would be like "building osmosis."

This concept of learning at least a modicum of hands-on experience in some physical trade is important for all of us. By learning how the things we use and on which we rely actually work, the veil of ignorance is lifted—even if only partially. This has become harder as we have become more reliant on technology, but not impossible. In some cases it might not seem to make sense to learn something due to the added cost, added time, or the complication of disposing of toxic waste that is produced from a task like changing the oil in your car, but I would still argue that one should learn to do it anyway. By actually getting your hands dirty and changing your oil, you allow your mind to lift the veil—ever so slightly—on your car's engine, and then the physical and the theoretical can merge.

CHAPTER 13

"To create, one must first question everything."
—Eileen Gray

After commencing work for Dave #2 and deciding to go it alone, I moved north to Santa Rosa, CA. I was out on my own for maybe six months working as an unlicensed architect and an unlicensed contractor when one day in the lumber yard, the tear-off informational display that I had seen a hundred times before from License Instruction Schools—a company that all but guarantees you will (eventually) pass your license exam and helps you through all of the minutia of actually becoming licensed—caught my attention. I had diligently ignored the display up until then, but that day the flier spoke to me. I tore one off and decided right then and there to get my general contractor's license. Between my degree in Urban Studies and Planning and my very brief career in building, I was just barely eligible for the exam. A couple of months and $1,000 later, I was sitting in the classroom cramming for my license exam.

The school provided a lot of material for you to study and learn on your own. They gave you binders and CDs with all the building code, safety, trade information, law—but most of it was pretty useless to me. The CDs basically present what amounted to a driving hazard because if you try listening to them in your car, you will fall asleep and crash (on the flip side, if you are looking for a cure for insomnia just talk to any contractor who got their license between ten and twenty years ago and ask if they still have the binder of CDs). The real value of the school, in my opinion, was the two day cram session that the school sets up for you on Saturday and Sunday before the Monday exam. Students spend two eight-hour sessions taking practice tests until their brains are so saturated with contract-specific information that when they look down at their dinner that evening, building codes fall out of their noses. The company all but guarantees you will pass the test, and if you don't, I believe they let you keep studying and re-taking the test at no extra charge. I still remember some weird and useless things from that test that I will never know why or how to implement. For example: How often do you need a cleanout on a masonry wall? Every six feet of course! I have no idea why a masonry wall would need a cleanout, nor have I ever run into a mason who had the foggiest idea of what I was talking about when I asked them the same question, but I passed that stupid test.

The real test that all contractors pass is the test of whether or not you can get your shit together enough to jump through the State License Board's hoops. A lot of guys screw up the application. One question in particular is a real killer: Have you ever been convicted of a crime? If you have had a DUI then the answer is yes. You can still get your license if the answer is yes, but if you answer no and you have had a DUI, then you are essentially lying on a State application and that makes Mongo mad.

I recall one of my employees asking me once, "Kelly, I'm thinking of getting my license. Will you sign off that you've seen my work over the last four years?"

I said, "Four years? I've only known you for one. And didn't you tell me you've only been in the trades for two?"

"Yeah," he responded with a look that said, 'Your point is...?'

I more or less played the same cards, and I figured if this guy can put it all together to get his license then he's probably got enough to be a fair-to-middling contractor. In California, the Contractor's State License Board (CSLB) is a division of the Consumer Protection Agency, so the reason they want contractors to be licensed is so they can control them, not so they can help them. They are not an agency set up to help contractors unless doing so helps consumers by proxy. Jumping through the contractor hoop is not hard, but it does create a very clear distinction between those with and those without. There is a weight that comes with the license. At least in California, it is a yoke that is made of paperwork held together by red tape. Guys doing work without a license might be looking over their shoulders more, but they are more able to do so because they can still turn their necks. Getting your license opens doors, but it also throws you into a dark and scary world of litigation, paperwork, and probably a world where you need to hire a bookkeeper and maybe even (God help you) employees. The CSLB is not there to help you with any of this, so if you ever have a problem, you have two people you can turn to: your fellow contractors and your attorney.

If you are going to make the effort to get your license, you are probably going to make a modest effort at professionalism. But I wonder if the bar of entry is set too low for entry into contractordom. Yes, setting the bar low makes it easy for trunk-slammers to go legit and trade in their Ford Escorts for Ford Rangers, but maybe we should demand much more from the people who are tasked with crafting our built environment. Maybe we craftsmen should demand more from ourselves—the way we did in a day-gone-by with apprenticeships for young up-and-coming talent, and reverence for builders as craftsmen. I can practically hear the eye-rolling from my builder cohorts, but I know they would agree that there are guys out there doing work who probably shouldn't be, and think that if we gave builders the esteem we give to other professionals, the trade would attract fewer losers. Nothing reminds me more of this fact of builder life than when I show up to a job, and the client says, "Kelly, I just want to thank you so much for showing up." I've heard it a number of times. Showing up? That's all I had to do to get your appreciation?

We should raise the standard we have in our hearts and our minds for the builder, but I am not recommending raising said bar through more strict licensing procedures. In fact, I think we would benefit from removing the licensing requirement all together. Licensing in the general contracting world is used to control contractors, not to ensure that they are competent. The license only guarantees that your contractor could jump through hoops, and serves as something that the Consumer Protection Agency can use as a stick. It does nothing to ensure quality or reliability, and at times provides a false sense of security for property owners. Much of the same could be said of architecture licenses, which serve as a membership to an exclusive club more so than any guarantee of competence.

Back in the day when builders were trained in apprenticeships, or less formally, simply learned from skilled masters, and building was a painstaking process, you could be reasonably sure you were getting what you paid for. When you look back now at the skilled work that builders did in years gone by, it is easy to marvel at perfectly bent radiuses in conduit, crown molding joined so tightly that you couldn't slip a piece of paper into the joint, or steel pipes fitted with rope and wax, all done without power tools. It is obvious that people executing those tasks were highly trained professionals. It's not a stretch to say that on average the men back in the day produced as high or higher quality work than we see today, and they did it all without being licensed by the CSLB. The evidence of their craftsmanship is all around us.

Regulation of the building industry actually prevents young people or unskilled workers from entering the profession at low levels. My own worker's compensation insurance, for example, is five times higher for lower wage workers than those who make over $30 per hour; incentivizing me, therefore, to hire more skilled labor rather than less. Unpaid internships are no longer a thing, and nobody wants to take the risk of hiring low-skilled workers who, if injured, can bring a whole world of hurt down on you from the State. As in all industries, if you raise the minimum wage or increase the cost of hiring unskilled people, companies will adapt to the situation by turning to technology or just hiring people who are highly trained and more experienced. The disincentives set in place to help the people at the bottom usually end up doing the opposite.

When I was just starting out on my own, I did a lot of

work without a license, permits, or insurance. My clients knew this, of course, and hired me for exactly those reasons. They didn't want a licensed contractor, a permit, or to pay for my insurance. They wanted a bathroom remodel or a non-loadbearing wall moved. I don't see why this should be a problem.

Take, for example, a job I did in San Francisco, where I added a wall to divide a very large master suite for a young lady. She wanted a three-way light switch added to the wall to control an existing fixture from two locations, rather than just the one. So I built the wall, ran the electrical, and finished the wall with drywall and paint. I may or may not have done everything 100% to the building code of the day. But she paid me a fraction of what it would have cost to do it with a license and permit, and so everyone was happy. Then let's say down the road she sells the house, and she discloses to the new owners that she did this wall and light switch with no permit. They acknowledge this and buy the house anyway and everyone is happy. Then let's say there is a fire that was started because I didn't staple the wiring in the wall but just left it loose (not sure that is really a thing, but let's just go with it for the sake of my gripping story). The new owner's insurance says, "We ain't paying," because the work was done without a permit. Seems fair enough to me.

If you want a cheap job done quickly but done well, you

have to cut corners somewhere, and if that means not getting a permit or hiring a licensed contractor, then in my humble opinion that should be your prerogative to do so. You made an agreement with your insurance company, and they are following the agreement. The builder, the homeowner, the buyer—everyone is in agreement on the work being done, and as long as nobody is lying to anybody else, there is no reason we can't choose to operate in this manner. What if people lie? Well, people do lie, and that is a problem, but not one that can be solved with permits and licenses.

It isn't only young ladies who are looking to cut corners and save on construction costs. Much like in any industry, there is a constant pressure to perform more tasks in less time. Technology has aided in that to a degree with things like power tools and advancing battery technology, but along with improved technology there has grown a demand for more work in less time, regardless of the quality. Building has become more and more expensive, especially in my home sweet home California, and so the temptation to cut corners and do things as cheaply as possible has only gotten stronger. Simultaneously, regulation of the building industry has only gotten more strict, which in turn makes building more expensive, and so the quality continues to suffer. It's a vicious cycle.

The difference between a house built in California in the

1860s and one built in the 1960s is staggering. Anyone who has ever embarked on a demolition project immediately notices that Victorian era homes used fatter lumber. A 2x4 at the turn of the century was two inches by four inches. The lumber industry changed that to 1.5 inches by 3.5 inches and overnight saved millions of board-feet of lumber; and coincidentally, the quality of homes built since then has steadily diminished. I don't think the extra half inch of lumber is indicative of quality in and of itself, but it is indicative of a key change where the building industry began looking for ways to do more with less. After World War II, America rushed to build housing for the booming population which was flocking to the suburbs. The quality of most quickly built homes in the 1950s and 1960s was horrible, and many have had to be retrofitted. A quick browsing of the many homes that claim to have set the world record for "Fastest House Ever Built!" on the internet will reveal the not-so-surprising truth that you cannot build a quality house in four hours.

Levittown, NY is probably the first and most notable suburban development where speed of construction was of utmost importance and where quality of craftsmanship took a backseat—or maybe even the trunk. Levitt and Sons, the firm who established Levittown, miraculously built one house every sixteen minutes at their peak, using assembly line manufacturing techniques from the auto industry. The builders used admittedly "unskilled" workers who went house to house performing one of twenty-six different specialized tasks (not skills), and installed components that came prefabricated from manufacturers. "We are not builders," said Levitt, the development's mastermind. "We are manufacturers."

This approach to building has stuck with us, and in some regards has been improved upon. The opportunity to blend the efficiencies introduced in the suburban land-rush of the '50s with higher quality materials and systems is there, but so is the draw to build structures as quickly as possible with the lowest skilled labor available. It is possible, for instance, to use factory-built trusses for your roof, or to introduce foam insulation, metal roofing, and high quality waterproofing. A conscious designer and diligent builder will ensure that that structure is built to last over a hundred years, but the same home put together with inferior materials and by the hand of an untrained worker could need retrofitting in as few as twenty.

In contrast, Victorians and Craftsman style homes that were built by hand in the nineteenth century have withstood the test of time. Many of those homes were built on foundations that didn't have steel rebar reinforcing, or were built right on the ground. My buddy Matt's parents' house was built in the late 1800s and was one such house that did not benefit from modern foundation technology, and in 1991 when Ferndale had three earthquakes in two days (all over 6.7 on the Richter scale), the post and pier foundation crumbled. Matt's two-story house fell to the ground and slid into the street. You might think this violent episode would ruin a house, but Matt's parents just lifted the house up, moved it into position, and bolted it down to a new and improved steel-reinforced foundation. Victorian homes were built to last, and incidentally, were done so in an era where building codes were not even twinkling in bureaucratic eyes.

I think this story is a testament to the quality of the craftsmanship of that era, and to the quality of the materials used. The builders of that house took their time building it because they had no other option. There were no time-saving technologies available that would allow an unskilled worker to rush through the mundane tasks. There were, however, unregulated apprenticeships in place which gave young men the chance to learn to be craftsmen of the future, and gave employers inexpensive labor. There were no lightweight sheet goods available back then to take the place of solid material, so builders were forced to precisely cut diagonal sheer blocking or diagonally placed solid wood sub-floor boards. Once new technologies were introduced that could save time and money, the race was on. Coupled with the advent of building codes and increased legislation of building practices, which added expense to building but did little to improve the building quality, only in the relatively rare case of the high end custom home, and with a uniquely patient and affluent homeowner, could the high standards of yesteryear be maintained.

Speaking of high standards, I once designed and built a bike shop in Sonoma for a guy named Jeff, who made his fortune selling tools that sharpened other tools that milled wood. His tools cost hundreds of thousands of dollars, so I imagine the actual milling tools for which his tools were designed to service must have cost a good bit more than that. Jeff had an eye for quality and all things German. One time I showed up to meet him in my wife's 1973 BMW 2002 and he went nuts. He ended up driving it that day, and if I had a mind to sell it I probably could have fleeced the guy. Jeff understood the value of quality and was willing to pay for it. I think his experience with tools and familiarity with the building material industry gave him insight that most normal people wouldn't have. It was a blast working for Jeff because he was not only a great guy, but held a wealth of knowledge on random topics that were always just outside the average person's experience. His bike shop was one of my best projects, but being a commercial project, time was of the essence, and we had a deadline. Jeff had to be open by April 1.

We modeled the shop itself after Jeff's concept of a typical German workshop, but with a wine country twist. We incorporated reclaimed wood from the floor of a sawmill (appropriate for a guy who made his fortune in that industry, I think), and mixed that medium with precision, steel, Stanley-Vidmar workshop cabinetry. It was a beautiful space and we were fortunate enough to be able to incorporate some custom furniture into it. The flagship piece was the Hub—a seven-sided display cabinet of wood, steel, and glass. I told my dad I was designing and fabricating a seven-sided piece of furniture and his response was, "Why would you do that?" His instinct was correct; seven-sided shapes are not for the timid. Seven is a prime number and just a bitch to figure out. If you think seven is a good idea, just do eight; no one will know the difference and the geometry will not be ridiculously difficult to decipher.

Jeff once told me and Matt a little story about milling machines. Since his machines sharpened the blades on the big milling machines, he had to know a lot about both. Jeff asked me once if I knew what kind of blades we used in the US for our different woods. I told him "Of course I do, but I don't like showing off, so why don't you tell me again."

So, he informed us that, "In the US we use diamond blades for our hardwoods, and we use carbide blades for our particle boards. The reason being that our hardwoods are clean, and the particle woods are generally made from the leftovers that are swept up off the floors of mills, and therefore contain a lot of contaminants like staples and broken teeth from saw blades.

"In Europe," Jeff continued, "they do the opposite. Their particle board is made from only specifically clean material so they use the diamond blades for that, but their hardwood comes from forests that have been through two world wars and is so full of shrapnel that it can't be milled without chewing up the machinery, so they use the carbide blades on that."

"Damn," Matt and I said simultaneously, our minds fully blown. I really respect that man; he gave me a few other tidbits that have stuck with me throughout my career. Jeff took a clinical and coldly efficient approach to running his bike shop business. The shop was basically his fun retirement hobby, but that didn't mean he didn't want to make money doing it.

Getting my contractor's license was a necessary, albeit painful, first step towards professionalism in the trades, but it took me a long time to learn how to make money in building. There is simply so much that can go wrong. Building quality homes, doing beautiful work, maintaining good vibes on a jobsite and a good relationship with your client, and hiring good employees and good subcontractors are all goals that you should have if you want to be successful, but all together are not enough to guarantee profit. If you don't have a really good guess as to what a project is going to cost before you begin, you will lose money on the project and everything I mentioned above—quality, beauty, good vibes, good relations, and keeping good folks working for you—will turn to shit. The pressure to be cheaper than the next guy will roll over a bright-eyed and inexperienced contractor like an unhitched trailer on a sloped driveway (there's a story there). That downward pressure has no bottom—you'll never be cheaper than Levittown. In order to be a profitable builder, you have to guess correctly about how much a job will cost, execute it in the period of time and with exactly as many mistakes (or fewer) as you anticipate, and convince your client that the cheaper bid from the other guy is a mirage.

By the way, we did get Jeff's bike shop open by April 1. Just to celebrate, I called up Matt early that morning and told him that someone had broken into our company shop and totally cleaned us out. "They took everything, man," I told him over the phone. Matt jumped in his truck and raced over to the shop. As he ran in, I could see him scanning the shelves and various storage areas in our shop doing a quick mental inventory of our tools. He could see they were all still in the places they were supposed to be and he then saw me standing there smiling and it hit him—April fucking Fool's Day. That was a good one.

CHAPTER 14

"If you want to get laid, go to college. If you want an education, go to the library."
—Frank Zappa

If you asked a kid what he wanted to do when he grew up and he said, "I wanna be a plumber," you'd probably think, 'Wow, this kid is a real loser,' but if that kid said, "I want to get a college degree so I can get an office job working for a corporation," he'd probably satisfy most of our current cultural expectations about what you should do when you grow up. In reality, that white-collar job comes with zero job security and way less pay than the plumber. And what is really so bad about a kid wanting to be a plumber? Sure, you might have to stand knee deep in human feces from time to time, but the money is good and people really need plumbers. No one ever said, "People really need regional sales managers." Not that the world doesn't need them, but why do we give that position higher status than the plumber? I think we have decided as a culture that to be a plumber is to be less-than. I think we would all benefit from a society-wide commitment to the trades as an honorable and respectable profession. We should be investing money and energy into trade schools and apprenticeships.

I know trade schools still exist, but their popularity has decreased over time. I think I know a way to have a private school that could be a self-sustaining enterprise. The way my scheme works goes like this: With initial capital investment, the school buys some land and/or a building and begins teaching the students by designing and building (or remodeling) a building, and then it sells or rents the finished product to fund the following session of education in the trades. Sure, the students are working for free, but they are actually getting a top-notch education in the trades, culminating in a high school diploma and perhaps a direct pipeline into the trades when they graduate. I call this the NCAA model, named after the National Collegiate Athletics Association who profit off student athletes and justify not paying them for their labor by asserting that they are receiving a free education. The major difference being that the trade school students would actually receive an education, and are much more likely to turn that education into a profession upon graduation.

If we could teach kids how to do their respective trades

with skill and pride, we could begin to reverse at least one aspect of a trend towards devaluating blue-collar careers. Kids graduating with an education in a trade would have pride in what they did for a living, rather than ending up in their trade because no matter how many times you get fired for drinking on the job, you can still find another drywall company who will hire you.

Take Germany as an example of how private investment in the blue-collar arts can actually contribute to the national economy. Manufacturing accounts for nearly a quarter of Germany's economic output, and Germany is the world's leading exporter of goods; they are revered around the world for their quality. In the US, manufacturing makes up only about 12%, and our stuff is not nearly as highly touted as German products are. The secret to Germany's success is Germany's apprenticeship training program that pumps out about half a million young German fabricators every year. They provide a steady stream of highly qualified blue-collar workers that helps Germany maintain its reputation for producing the best stuff in the world.

Another area where I see room for improvement is in the technology of the building field. The technology on most jobs is pretty much the same no matter where you go, and has been for a long time. With the exception of some battery technology which has replaced all but the most powerful power tools, there is very little innovation happening on construction sites, and the same can be said for the industry at large. For whatever reason, technological advancements in the building industry have been slow to catch on. In the last ten thousand years we have gone from the hammer and nail to the pneumatic nail gun—not exactly mind-blowing. On Dave's jobsite we had nail guns of course, but by and large we framed the whole house by hand with hammer and nails just like they did in Egypt back in 3400 BC. In fact, even the siding contractor on the Kentfield job who meticulously covered every square inch of the building's exterior with cedar shingles used a hammer and nails (his pace was actually quite impressive). In case that didn't blow your mind, I am going to repeat it: he covered the entire exterior of a two story, 4,500 square foot home with cedar shingles using a hammer and nails—boom.

On a micro level, advances in technology in the trades is hampered by the resistance that one encounters from conventional wisdom. The head honchos of most small firms, who would otherwise be the ones to implement changes to the way things are done, are very unlikely to do so when *it's the way things have always been done.* "My father did it this way and his father before him" attitudes are common in the industry. Attempts to implement a new way of doing things will almost always be met with skepticism, and even ridicule. Building trades are run by many small bands of native builders, not giant corporations, so there is no easy mechanism to introduce new ideas.

One area that I have had direct experience of the resistance to change is in the Energy Performance movement. This concept of treating the house like a high performance dwelling machine is not all together new, but recently a more scientific approach has rejuvenated interest in Energy Performance. In a nutshell, Energy Performance is approaching the construction of a building using a verifiable method to make homes more energy efficient. By implementing Energy Performance methods and then testing the home to see the actual results of the work performed, the Energy Performance movement has thrown a lot of conventional wisdom out the double-hung, single-glazed window.

I can hear the old-school HVAC guys now: “My ductwork has always been tighter than a gnat’s ass.”

“How do you know?” I might respond.

“Because I’ve been doing it my whole life. I know how to run tight ductwork!”

When put to the test, even the most conscientious HVAC installer was not running tight ductwork and had to modify their techniques. This had led to changes in the energy code in California, and now all ductwork must be tested for airtightness.

The name of the game in most instances of improved

energy performance in a house is airtightness. Most inefficiencies come down to air leakage—whether in HVAC ducts, doors and windows, or the building envelope itself. This idea flies directly in the face of the conventional wisdom that you hear repeated all over the place: "houses need to breathe." Houses do not need to breathe. They are not mammals, they are buildings. They should be energy efficient and built to last. Old leaky houses need to breathe because they are leaky. If water gets into the walls of your old Victorian Painted Lady, then the fact that there is no insulation and plenty of air flow (not to mention old-growth redwood or cypress lumber) in those walls will ensure that the water dries out quickly and does no damage. New houses should not breathe; they should be so tight that spiders can only enter through the front door while you are carrying in your groceries.

Most people's ideas about energy efficiency in houses is misinformed because it comes from stupid marketing campaigns. Window manufacturers have convinced us that our old single-pane windows are draining our bank accounts, when actually new double-pane windows are only slightly more insulated than the single-pane variety. The real issue is typically air leakage around the windows, and so installing a new window means you are usually sealing up the area around the window just by nature of removing and replacing the opening in your wall. Ceiling fan manufacturers have convinced us that ceiling fans will actually cool off our houses. This is nonsense. A fan is a motor that is generating heat and only makes you feel cool if you are standing under it. The fan does not cool anything down but your skin through evaporation, and the heat from the motor actually adds to the overall temperature of your house, costs money to operate, and probably cost more to install than you thought. Solar manufacturers have convinced us that we need a Porsche on our roofs, when we actually need bicycles. Did you know that $1 spent on an energy-efficient lightbulb replacement will save as much energy as $9 of solar will generate? But admittedly, solar is sexy, and of course we need solar, but we also need to save energy and that story is not usually told.

From a macro level, technological advances in building have not been quick to emerge either. One area that seems like it would be promising is in factory-built buildings, but the products that come out of factories today are pretty much the same thing that comes out of a site-built structure, the main difference being that there is less waste. Buildings built in factories are not built by robots, or made out of new-fangled materials, or 3D printed, or any other crazy technology; they are built by low wage workers with nail guns and pneumatic glue dispensers on a (sort of) assembly line. So, for now the Great American Contractor is still relevant. There is no way to outsource home building and repair, and the robots have not yet replaced carpenters, plumbers, or electricians.

So if your kid tells you he wants to be a plumber when he grows up, don't freak out. Sure, that's a little weird, but how about celebrating the fact that that career choice will probably be a lucrative one with all the job security you could ever ask for. And maybe consider sending him to my private school for the trades so he can be prepared for the world of pipe fitting and not simply end up there. Give your young person who is bound to end up in the trades all the tools and lessons that a grizzled old plumber has learned in a lifetime up front, so he can hit the ground running. The building profession is not for the meek, and it will chew you up and spit you out if you're not prepared for the abuse that is heading your way.

There is a sign in my local blueprint printing shop that you can purchase for $25 that captures this admittedly cynical sentiment. It reads:

> Construction Terms Defined
>
> Contractor–A gambler who never gets to shuffle, cut, or deal.
>
> Bid Opening–A poker game in which the losing hand wins.
>
> Bid–A wild guess carried out to two decimal places.
>
> Low Bidder–A contractor who is wondering what he left out.
>
> Engineer's Estimate–The cost of construction in heaven.
>
> Project Manager–The conductor of an orchestra in which every musician is in a different union.
>
> Critical Path Method–A management technique for

losing your shirt under perfect control.

OSHA–A protective coating made by half-baking a mixture of fine print, red tape, split hairs, and baloney—usually applied at random with a shotgun.

Strike–An effort to increase egg production by strangling the chicken.

Delayed Payment–A tourniquet applied at the pockets.

Completion Date–The point at which liquidated damages begin.

Liquidated Damages–A penalty for failing to achieve the impossible.

Auditor–Person who goes in after the war is lost and bayonets the wounded.

Lawyer–Person who goes in after the auditors to strip the bodies.

I recall seeing that sign for the first time and thinking, 'Well that sure is a cynical perspective.' I was probably less than two years into my contracting career at that point, and was like Bambi—all bright eyed and unaware of cruelty lurking around every corner. Now I look at that sign and think, 'Why isn't that sign posted in every kindergarten in America?'

Somehow, as Americans we have fostered an environment where in order to build anything, whether it be a dog house or a hospital, you have to enter into an arrangement with someone that seems more like a poker game than a mutually beneficial business transaction. Part of the reason for this is that we have unrealistic expectations of our builders. We expect builders to know exactly how much time and money it is going to take to do something no one has ever done before, and we expect them to compete against other builders who have never done the job before, have no formal training in building, and might be on their way out of business.

When you take your car to a mechanic, you must pay her first to do a diagnostic of what is wrong with your vehicle (granted, some kind-hearted mechanics will not charge you for this, but you can bet your Ford or Chevy dealer will). Then you get an estimate for what it is going to cost to replace, say, your alternator. That cost is based on an actual book that says how many hours it will take to do various tasks. This number is calculable because there are thousands of cars with that same alternator, installed the same way, and thousands of mechanics who have done the change out in near identical fashion. Then, if something goes wrong—say the mechanic breaks a bolt off inside the threaded mount and has to spend extra time to remove that bolt—you pay for the extra time. It is all very clear and not disputable. And then, if you don't pay your mechanic, she gets to keep your car.

Contrast that with a contractor who you have hired to do a remodel/addition on your house. Your house is unique. Even if you live in a tract development with cookie-cutter homes that are all alike, there are often subtle differences from house to house due to changes homeowners have made over the years, or custom options that people opted for during building, or problems that have arisen during the life of the home. Your builder has to make educated guesses about how your house was built and what is going on inside your walls. Then there is the moving target your builder has to hit around weather, holidays, employee needs, and acts of God, all of which can cause delays or problems of their own—none of which are acceptable excuses in the minds of homeowners who are coughing up what usually amounts to a small fortune. And lastly, your builder has to deal with you. You might be a totally rational actor, or you could be an emotional nutjob—no one knows until they get to spend some time with you. You have desires, opinions, and expectations that (for the six months it takes to complete your project) your builder has to try to accommodate, understand, or ignore. And God forbid you and your spouse are not on the same page, and end up using the remodel of your home as a venue for divorce proceedings. Your house is not a Ford. No one has ever done your addition or your remodel before, and therefore has no idea what it is actually going to take to remodel your home.

Consider the medical trade in juxtaposition to the building trade: Have you ever tried to ask your doctor what your doctor visit was going to cost you? He will just look at you inquisitively like you asked him a question about the best method for storing holiday leftovers. Doctors are among the most well-respected professions in the world, and yet have no idea how much his trade costs his clients. Go ahead and ask him how much something like surgery or an MRI will cost. You will most likely get a laugh out of your doctor with a ridiculous question like that.

When your bill arrives for a medical procedure, the amount owed is always a surprise. Imagine what it would be like if we built homes the way we do health care in the US. Your "New House" bill would arrive with an astronomical number that you had no intention of ever paying in the first place, and certainly would have entertained other options had you known you would be out of pocket so much money. Then, two days later, you receive another bill that was from the builder for his fee, that "obviously" was not included in the bill for the house. You have to pay the builder separately for his services.

Similar to the above example, I think homeowners often feel like the total cost for their home or whichever level of project was more in the end than they were promised in the beginning. The difference here, though, is that nine times out of ten a project takes longer and costs more than initially conceived. This can be due to overly optimistic estimating from the contractor, but often results from changes by the homeowner to the original scope of work. It seems silly, but it's been my experience that most homeowners don't understand that those changes cost more money and take more time. I think this issue is probably due more to human nature than to malice or ignorance, but I also think there is room for improvement in the way we conceive of building projects and contracts between parties.

We expect builders to put themselves in perilous positions every time they take on a project. No other professionals are expected to be so financially leveraged as builders who may be on the hook for tens of thousands of dollars at a time in materials, wages, and subcontractor invoices. It doesn't take much for a contractor to get into a bad situation where his only option is bankruptcy—it happens all the time. Which is why you have probably heard stories of contractors using the deposit from one job to pay for another job. A good friend of mine who works as a project manager for a high-end builder on multi-million dollar projects once told me about subcontractors going bankrupt during the job. He said that he's seen contractors close up shop, reopen under a different name, and then come back onto the same job and finish what they started under a new contract. He says it happens all the time.

I don't think this is the best way for us to build our homes nor our communities. I believe at the core of the problem is a shared attitude towards builders. If we respected the building trade like we respect doctors, then we would encourage young people to learn a trade, study it, go to school for it, and thereby we would produce a professional workforce. We would expect success from these highly trained professionals and they would in turn hold themselves to a higher standard. It was not that long ago when we had some basic modicum of esteem for our builders and at least sent them through apprenticeships. Today we dump people who can't speak English, or who couldn't get into college, or simply don't work well with others into the trades as a last resort. We don't value the blue-collar professions at large, and as in all things, we get what we pay for.

Why not pay your builder on a Time and Materials basis? Time and Materials, or T&M, means you pay for the amount of time plus the cost of materials. There are variations on this theme where you might pay the builder his costs (T&M) plus a lump sum for profit, or his time plus a markup on the materials only, but the basics are the same: You pay for what it costs to build your building. I have found that many clients are weary of the T&M contract because it seems like a blank check for the contractor to run wild with no regard for the client's budget. This is understandable if you don't know your builder very well, or don't trust your builder, or just can't spend the time and energy to monitor his work. But if you do know your builder, and you trust that he is working for you and in your best interests—protecting your budget as if it were his own—then why not pay him exactly what it costs to build the project? T&M is the fair option. Both parties pay and receive exactly what they owe and deserve respectively. It is true that if your contractor makes a minor mistake you have to pay for the fix, but mistakes happen, and in a bid situation any smart contractor has a contingency in the bid to take care of any unforeseeable complications or mistakes. In the bid scenario, if those mistakes don't happen, you are paying for them anyways.

When you choose a contractor to build your project you are essentially entering into a six-month-long relationship with a stranger. This person will be interacting with you on a daily basis, talking to you, calling you at night, receiving calls from you over the weekend, asking you for money, getting to know you (inside your home) on a very personal level. Why would you choose this person solely based on their initial gamble on how much it will cost them to build your dreams? That's like choosing a spouse solely based on their tax return—which happens, I know—but what a shitty way to find a spouse. Furthermore, why would anyone choose the contractor with the lowest, and often most unrealistic, estimation? Is that really what you want? The cheapest possible product? Unless you are assuming that they have underbid the project and are likely to lose their shirt on the job, but just don't care. Again, that is a shitty way to start a relationship with someone. T&M contracts take all of the guesswork out of the beginning of the project, and instead empower the contractor to work within a budget. It is reasonable, and very helpful, to have an estimate of what the project will cost, and also to be very transparent as to what you are paying for: How much do the workers make? How much does the contractor pay herself? Where are the materials coming from? How do we save money in order to achieve the mutual goal of building your building within your budget? Of course, no contractual system is impervious to things going sideways. However, in my experience the relationship should be the governing factor, and the contract should only be a framework upon which that relationship is built.

Speaking of a T&M project going sideways, here is one nightmarish example I can share from my own experience: Once, I was approached by a close family friend to help out his close friend with a seismic retrofit. This close family friend was an attorney. His friend was in trouble with the county for building a two-story addition on her house with no permit, and I found out later that our close family friend owed her a hefty chunk of change. This client lived in a filthy house. Her house was occupied by herself and two giant, long-haired dogs. Dishes piled sky high in the kitchen, junk everywhere–one of the rooms in her house was so piled with crap you couldn't enter–and when I forced open the door to look inside the room was filled with spiderwebs so thick, it was like a horror movie. These factors were warning signs that a more experienced me would have noticed and avoided like smallpox. All of this should have made me think twice about entering into a contract (relationship) with this lady, but I was young and inexperienced (still paying tuition).

The project itself was very complicated and we were not the first contractors to attempt it. In fact, we had to fix some mistakes by the previous builder, who attempted to remedy the situation along with the retrofitting of the original unpermitted construction. We first had to remove the "cinder block" foundation, which in the most seismically active zones in California might as well be milk crates, and replace it with reinforced concrete and sheer systems that extended from the ground to the roof. All of this had to be done within the walls of an existing house. In order to pull this off, we had to brace the house in place while demolishing the crap foundation below. While the house was suspended in the air, we formed a new foundation of concrete and steel. Inside the first and second floors of the building, we opened the walls and installed steel rods, specially designed sheer wall systems, and hardware to anchor the house to the new foundation below. It was not an easy job. It required brute strength to jackhammer concrete out of the crawlspace, and precision to line everything up so the whole system would work together.

Because of the complexity of the job, both parties agreed that T&M was the appropriate way to proceed. To make a long story short, when we were about 75% complete with the project, she decided to quit paying us. I had let billing lapse for about two weeks, and due mostly to bad timing, the amount she owed us had grown to around $32,000. Despite our on-time and on-budget performance of her very complicated project, she came to the conclusion that we were not owed what we were asking for. No matter how hard I tried to explain that we were performing exactly what we agreed to, there was no reasoning with her, and so we were left with no choice but to take her to court. Guess who represented her in our arbitration hearing? If you guessed the close-family-friend-attorney-guy, you would be correct. The moral of the story here is that T&M is no substitute for trust. This client did not trust us. I know this because it came out in the hearing that she was secretly videotaping us while we worked.

It is no wonder people hate attorneys. Even today, I still can't believe that the close-family-friend-attorney-guy would trade his close (and potentially lucrative, but that's a story for another time) friendship with our family for whatever he was getting from his friend—money? Looking back, I think they might have had it out for us from the start. In the end, though, we won our dispute and she had to pay above what she originally owed us—somewhere in the ballpark of $50,000 for our attorney's fees, the work itself, and interest. Even though we were right, and we knew all along were doing a good job on her project, and we were eventually vindicated by the court, there is only bitterness in my memory of that project. If I had the whole thing to do over again, I would have taken note of the warning signs that were evident from the beginning and I would not have entered into that relationship. I should correct what I said about attorneys; in truth, people only hate other people's attorneys. I love my attorney, and consider him one of the most decent human beings I have ever had the pleasure of knowing. It almost makes me not want to tell jokes about attorneys, but I know he loves lawyer jokes, so here's one for Jack:

What's the difference between a dead lawyer in the middle of the road and a dead skunk? The skunk has skid marks in front of it.

I mentioned before that the best training for a contractor would be a law degree. The reason for that is that the contract exists solely for the purpose of keeping you from getting sued, or to help you win a lawsuit if you do get sued. A contract originally was intended just to show your client what you were going to do, and how much they were going to pay for said work. My own contract is eight pages long now and has been edited multiple times by different attorneys. It's full of all sorts of disclaimers and back doors and ways for me to wiggle out of promises I never made. I don't like it, but I'd be crazy to go into agreements with people without it. A handshake is fine, but if you are going to put it in writing, then you better make sure you have an iron-clad contract.

One last thing about attorneys. Contractors have very good reason to be weary of attorneys, especially in California. I have a contractor friend who is also a lawyer, and he told me about a seminar that he went to about window flashing lawsuits. I had heard something once about how the majority of construction lawsuits were for improperly flashed windows. I thought at the time that this must have been due to window installers doing a shitty job, but what my lawyer-turned-contractor friend told me was that, actually, lawyers had developed a technique for shaking down contractors where they would get their clients to claim that windows were leaking or simply to state that they "thought" the windows were improperly flashed, and that they should sue their contractor. The only way to fight the lawsuit was to pull apart the window, siding, and trim, and show everyone how the window was flashed. At that point it would be anyone's guess as to whether the window had been flashed correctly or not, as there are a dozen different techniques, none of which have ever been scientifically tested, and the act of tearing the window/trim assembly apart would likely ruin the flashing as well. Most no-nonsense contractors didn't want to go to the trouble, and so they would just let their liability insurance provider settle. It was a total shakedown.

So the moral of the story is: Avoid other people's attorneys, or become one yourself, or become a plumber. The jobsite could be a place we are proud to send our sons and daughters, but it needs work. We need to reevaluate our relationship with builders and consider them worthy of the respect we give other professionals. We need to train them with that same respect in mind, and in turn raise our expectations of them and the building industry at large. I'm going to get started with my private school for the trades, and if anyone has any ideas for the curriculum, I'm all ears.

CHAPTER 15

"A camel is a horse designed by committee."
—Sir Alec Issigonis

There was a time long ago when builders were architects and architects were builders. Throughout most of human history, the person who designed your mud hut was also the person who built it. By the way, depending on where you live, you may or may not have run into a cob building, bench, or other structure. Cob is essentially a mud and straw mixture that gets formed into a desired shape, usually by hand. Around Sonoma County they are quite prevalent and, frankly, they all suck. I have never seen one done that didn't look like it was built by a drunk four-year-old. Can we stop with the free-form, sloppy finish, earthy, crunchy cob building? I mean, the technology might actually be fine, but why does it have to be this gross turd-shaped and turd-colored blob? Would it kill you to put it in a form or use some tools to make it look halfway intentional?

Sorry, I just had to get that off my chest. So, yes, back in the day if you wanted a new house, you went to an architect to have it designed and built. Nowadays you still might start with an architect, but you then must also hire a builder. The two-headed monster that is our current system is not ideal. Because architects are no longer builders, they tend not to design with the builder in mind like they did when they were one in the same. And, because the builders of today are generally cynical men who have been hardened by a life of manual labor, carrying heavy shit, and consistently injuring themselves, they tend to be suspicious of architects who wear stylish eyeglasses and mostly work indoors. A gap has developed between the two fields.

I think the perceived sentiment held by your typical builder is that architects are fond of designing things that cannot be built, and because they wear clean shoes they are members of the cultural elite who look down their noses at dirty, stinking contractors. That attitude towards architects might not be universal or even totally deserved, but it is not uncommon. I once had a professor who was an architect, and also had a general contractor's license. He would tell us that whenever he went onto a jobsite the first thing he would do was tell the builders that he was a "GC" just so they would let down their guards a bit. I take a different approach. When I show up on a jobsite—being secure in my building prowess (read: manhood)—I wear nice clothes and nice shoes; that way no one ever asks me to hold the end of a board or pick up anything heavy, but I always drive my beater pickup truck with lumber racks, and I always, always bring a bag of cracked pepper sunflower seeds. Nothing says "I'm just as much man as you" like skillfully spitting out sunflower seed shells.

There is a way of building that I believe is better. It is called: design-build (cue music). Why is it better? Glad you asked. I said before that our current system is a two-headed monster. It is actually a five-headed monster: architect, engineer, builder, homeowner, municipality. Sometimes the lender or insurance company also has a say in how things are done, which makes it a six-headed monster. God forbid if the homeowners are a couple who both have opinions as to how to do things, but don't actually communicate with one another—not only does that add another head to the monster (it's a sub-head really, but still dangerous), it also turns the project into a really long and expensive counseling session. There's nothing like installing crown molding while trying to mediate a lover's quarrel.

Design-build merges the builder and the architect, and largely, the engineer; much the way things were done in the old days. You used to hire an architect to literally build you a house. By merging designers and builders, you cut off two of the six heads, and as people always say, "four heads are better than six." The design-build method is a more efficient model because from the beginning, the project is being designed with construction in mind. During the construction phase, any oversights by the designer are handled with very little fuss, and the same is true for changes. If a client wants to move a window, for example, we just move it, and if a new drawing is needed I make a new drawing; if the engineer needs to be involved I can simply call him up, describe the situation, and more often than not get a verbal "okay" to proceed. The whole process from change of mind to beginning execution of said change can take mere minutes, and all parties are on board immediately. In the typical architect-designed building, when the client walks into their home during the framing phase and realizes that the pantry is too small or the windows need adjusting, the homeowner will start their appeal process with whichever carpenter is standing closest to them at the moment. From there the communication moves up the step ladder to the foreman or the general contractor, who informs the homeowner that they will have to get approval and new drawings from the architect and the engineer—not to mention a change order from all three. Meanwhile, the carpenters are probably standing around looking at each other wondering if they should be picking loose nails up off the floor. Design-build leaves room for these changes without wasting time or money.

What the architect-designed model assumes is that a fully conceived project can be presented to and understood by your typical homeowner (and builder) prior to commencement of construction. This means that you should be able to understand how your home will look and feel, and your builder will understand how it will be constructed based on a dozen drawings and a few three-dimensional renderings (usually printed in 2D). This is a fantasy, and every project ever conceived has had issues come up in the construction that didn't occur to the designer during the design phase—it is just the way God made the world. No matter how robust the designs are, they are still just two-dimensional representations of an actual space. The great Pete Perisic once said, "Always make a model," and I believe he was right, but even a model is not a substitute for the real thing.

There are things that my friends and I have come to call "the actuals." There are the plans, and there are the actuals. The actuals exist in the gray area where the two-dimensional representation of three-dimensional space cannot actually convey all the information of what is actually happening in a building. This situation is especially prevalent in remodels/additions where the builder is marrying new structure to old. It is nearly impossible to figure out exactly how engineering details and connections between surfaces will work before the existing house is opened up and stripped down to its bare essentials. Fortunately, in the design-build method, we can adopt a wait and see approach in which we figure out minor and major details in the field after we have established a basic direction on our basic plans. This might sound like a "make it up as you go" approach to building, and well, it is.

The design-build building is conceived by a practical-minded artist who does not live merely in the abstract, but who has intimate knowledge of the way their art gets pieced together. You might think I'm throwing around the word artist a bit willy nilly here, and to be sure not all design-builders would refer to themselves as artists, but I would argue that building design is at the very least a branch on the art tree. Designing a house is a very practical art, but art nonetheless.

When I am hired to build a home for someone, I almost always leave a substantial number of details undecided until the time of implementation. I have been accused of having "sparse" plans before (not intended as a compliment). This is intentional. Usually these belated decisions don't require a change in engineering or permitting, but can be left up to the discretion of the skilled tradesperson who is implementing the change, or the whim of the homeowner. However, there are times when a decision on some detail which is put off ends up requiring new drawings or the approval of an engineer or building official. This is usually anticipated and can be handled with ease and efficiency by the same person who is implementing the change—namely me.

Design-build is a higher form of building. When coupled with a T&M contract and advanced technology, the result is a better way to build. We have been building houses in the same way for centuries, so by advanced technology, I mean looking for new ways to build that are pushing the limits of efficiency, aesthetics, and economy. I have been developing a home concept that uses premanufactured steel structures in a customizable system. This approach saves a ton of time and money, and the end product is beautiful. The pretty drawings that I have been creating with this system are some of the most interesting concepts that I have ever done, and have also led to the best experiences I have ever had with my clients.

CHAPTER 16

"The physician can bury his mistakes, but the architect can only advise his client to plant vines."—Frank Lloyd Wright

Before reaching the state of pure bliss that I am currently working in, I had my moments of doubt. I had been contracting for about seven years with two different partners, Mike and Matt, when the day came where I heard myself utter the words, "I hate my job." My former partner Mike had come to that same conclusion two years prior, and he decided enough was enough, so he went to work for a big building firm as a project manager. When I heard myself say those words I figured, I did not want to be the kind of person who trudges through life hating his job, so I followed suit and closed the doors on my firm EPIC Design-Build.

My next move would be to go back to work for someone

else. Luckily a friend offered me a job managing his landscaping crews, so I took it. The feeling, that first week, of coming home at 5:00 p.m., opening a beer, and not giving another moment's thought to my job was nothing short of ecstasy. Eventually I got used to the feeling, but that first week I felt like the luckiest man on earth: I had made it out alive.

Up until that point my only experience with landscaping was watching the landscapers from a distance on various jobs of mine. Whenever landscaping came up in a conversation, Matt or I would always throw out the line, "Do Mexican landscapers listen to the Scorpions?" The line comes from a time when Matt and I were leaving a house we were working on, and the landscaping crew, all Mexican dudes, were working out front. Before we got to the front of the house we could hear their music, and it was not what we were expecting. Nine times out of ten when you hear the music from an all Mexican landscaping crew you will hear Mexican music—usually ranchera or banda. This day was different, and Matt and I looked at each other before we opened the front door and at the same time said, "Is that the Scorpions?" The crew were blasting "Rock You Like a Hurricane," and when I asked them if that was their iPod they were listening to, they said, "Yeah," with a look that said, 'So what?' From then on, any time Matt or I asked a question where the obvious answer was yes, the response would be, "Do Mexican landscapers listen to the

Scorpions?" Of course they do.

Speaking of music on jobsites, most workplaces—construction or otherwise—that I have experienced have had music playing throughout the day or night. What type of music depends on the nature of the work being done. In the Hallmark store where I worked that one holiday season—I can't even bring myself to talk about that music. Almost every job has its corresponding sound track. It's almost a cliché that surgeons play classical or jazz music during operations, and while not exactly brain surgery, building sites are no melodic exception. Not sure if it is the same in other parts of America, but in California you hear three types of music on jobsites; unless of course you are working for a cosmic carpenter who will most likely be playing some hipster band that you have never heard of, or if he is a real trippy dude he'll make everyone listen to classical, or even jazz (I know, "What are you, a brain surgeon?"). But by and large, in California you hear country music (new stuff, never the good stuff), classic rock (radio station, commercials and all), or banda/ranchera Mexican music.

I guess I was always a classic rock guy, and so was my first boss Dave. We used to sing at the top of our lungs on his job, and to this day we still send each other text messages with the nothing but the word "Science!" in reference to the song "She Blinded Me with Science." Classic rock is an uplifting, relatively fast pace genre that lends itself to tape measurer air guitar solos. Sure it gets old, and I never need to hear "Hotel California" or "Stairway to Heaven" again as long as I live, but it's also comforting, which is I think the appeal of banda to Latino dudes.

According to a statistic I made up just now, 90% of all music played on jobsites in California is Mexican music, and sometimes you will hear two radios playing two different Mexican music stations at the same time. This is the classic condition of dueling radios. This is a dangerous situation, especially if you are epileptic or have a family history of strokes. Dueling radios is not a rare phenomenon. I have had to tell people to turn off their radios on more than one occasion because they were pissed off at one trade or another for some stupid reason, and were taking it out on everyone by trying to out-music the offender.

Nowadays I rarely find myself listening to music, and when I walk onto a jobsite the first thing I do is turn off whatever radio is playing. I don't have the tolerance to shout or to strain to hear over "More Than a Feeling" while talking to my fire sprinkler contractor about how I need to design my houses around the sprinkler system so he can feel respected. I don't know if I am just getting old, or maybe it is the immense weight of the world on my shoulders that prevents me from relaxing enough to enjoy music on a jobsite these days; either way, it is rare that I listen to music while working. I see my dad doing it in his shop, and I think 'That looks nice, maybe I'll do that when I am in my golden years.'

One time, Matt and I were remodeling the home for one of our favorite clients of all time, Kerry, and despite her terrific attitude, her taste in music was not in line with mine nor Matt's. Nothing against people who are, but we are not what you would call Dave Matthews Band fans. One afternoon Matt was doing the drywall taping and texturing of the three skylights we installed in Kerry's living room. This was an excruciating job because even though it was not a hot day, it was a sunny day. Inside the light wells that surround the skylight the temperature can get quite high, and the brightness of the white walls is almost unbearable. So, Matt is up on the ladder working and sweating his balls off while cursing under his breath when Kerry runs into the living room exclaiming, "Dave Matthews Band!" and cranks the radio up. Knowing how much Matt hated Dave Matthews, I just started laughing and left the room for the cool calm of the front yard.

Where was I? Ah yes, landscaping is fun.

I really enjoyed the two years I spent leading the landscaping crews. I love working outdoors. I love working with plants. If you ever get a chance to work in a nursery, I recommend it. One of my favorite jobs ever was working in a nursery in San Diego. Nursery employment probably won't pay well, but you will learn a lot about plants and it is a usually a laid-back environment, and guaranteed to be populated with young, beautiful people.

Okay, no more distractions. After closing my design-build firm and joining up with the landscaping company, I found myself in a really good mood. I was fortunate to be involved in some beautiful projects and got to do a ton of tractor work, which I love. I had a few assignments where I designed and built small steel structures and just felt fairly free. I really gained a lot of valuable skills and knowledge of systems, like low voltage lighting and irrigation. You might think that the level of excitement on a landscaping crew would be low, but you'd be wrong. Crazy shit happens on landscaping jobs the same way it does on regular old building jobs.

Once, while doing a really beautiful modern landscape installation, I had a trailer full of mulch parked in our client's driveway. The driveway was gently sloped uphill away from the street. It is always a good practice to "chock" the tires of a trailer when it is not hooked up to a truck—even on flat ground. This was not flat ground, and whoever unhooked the trailer and moved the truck did not chock the tires, so the trailer was sitting there not moving only by the friction of the trailer jack sitting on the driveway. The plate at the base of the jack was well-abused from years of landscapers beating the hell out of the trailer. Every time the trailer scraped a driveway or hit a rock, the plate got bent up a little bit so that now it was curved up like the front of a waterski.

So there the trailer sits, precariously perched on a sloped driveway with the friction of a waterski on gravel holding it in place, when I begin to raise the dump bed and dump the mulch. I got about halfway up and before any mulch had fallen out, the trailer broke free from the minimal friction that was holding it in place and began to roll down the driveway and into the street—trailer jack just skiing along in the front like an '80s speedboat advertisement. I let go of the dump bed controller, unable to do anything to stop this two-ton battering ram from careening towards the neighbor's steel fence across the street, and as it hits the neighbor's planter strip between the street and the fence, the weight of the trailer digs the jack into the soil and begins plowing through the planter. It rips up the logs along the edge of the planter, the irrigation, and a number of plants, and only by the grace of God stops one inch from the fence. It was a miracle that it didn't hit the fence and do damage that I couldn't fix with a crack team of highly skilled landscapers.

Everyone immediately stopped what they were doing and jumped into action to fix this fucked up situation. We used a tractor to drag the trailer out and back across the street (chocked the tires this time), replanted all of the plants that had been plowed out of the ground, put the logs back in place around the planter, and fixed all of the broken irrigation. We spread a little mulch around and in about ten minutes, the whole planter looked like nothing had happened. The neighbors were never the wiser. That crew saved my bacon that day because even though I was not the one who disconnected the trailer from the truck, I should have checked to make sure the trailer was safe before lifting the dump bed. I'm lucky I was in charge of a landscaping crew that day and not there doing carpentry.

As much fun as I was having in landscaping, my time there did not last. After about two years, I got an offer from a builder friend to manage one of his crews. He was willing to pay me much more than I was making landscaping and I couldn't say no. I worked for that friend for about a year when I got another offer that I couldn't refuse, and so I moved on again, and this time I was seduced back out on my own.

The new gig was to design and build a gigantic house. The project included work to the vast property as well, which all told, amounted to an enormous undertaking—especially for just one man. In order to handle such a big job, I needed to put down my tool belt and don my project manager belt (it's nice—huge brass belt buckle). With the new gig I changed my business name to Kelly Cowan Designs, and I also changed my way of building things. I no longer engaged in much physical work, but in order to stay ahead of the curve on such a big project, I supervised other people's work and showed them how to execute the plans that I designed.

For the most part that approach worked pretty well on that job, although the client insisted on using cheap unskilled labor as much as possible. Every time I wanted to bring in a professional subcontractor, the client would argue that her "crew" could probably do the task with my supervision. I would argue that, "Yes, they probably could do it, but I am going to have to show them how to do every little step, then we'll have to go back and fix everything they screw up, and then we will still end up with a slightly inferior product." Call me old-fashioned, but if I am a rich millionaire building my dream home, I am hiring the best people to build it. I got frustrated trying to manage people who didn't really want to work. I caught one of the "crew" sleeping under the house once and I wasn't even mad. I just thought, 'You don't have it. You never will. Just stay down here under the house and don't get in anyone's way.'

I am always mystified by how slowly people are capable of working. Why go slow? At the end of the day, you get paid the same amount whether you are working fast or slow; it's not like it's easier to mope around a jobsite. I get it if you don't want to be here, but just go do something else and stop wasting everyone's time and money. One day I was near my wit's end managing the "crew," and I saw this guy Mick walking down the long driveway to his truck. "Where's Mick going?" I asked.

"I think he's going to get his tape measurer," answered the guy up on the ladder.

"What a novel idea," I said, "a tape measurer on a jobsite. Next thing you know he'll be carrying it around with him, and then maybe a pencil and even a hammer!" If you are on the jobsite there is no reason in hell for your tape measurer to be in your truck—unless you are in your truck with it. Even if I did find myself without a tape measurer in my bags or on my tool belt for some completely inconceivable reason, I would not walk to my truck to get it; I would run, and so should you.

Another thing that drives me absolutely nuts on a jobsite is when I see guys talking but not working. You can do both. My mantra on every jobsite where I am in charge of other humans is, "Lips moving, hands moving." Talk all you want, but don't stop working.

My attitude has always been: If there is a faster way to do something, I will find it. I will always take the shortest path from A to B, I will constantly search for shortcuts, and I will always look for the easy way out of every problem I encounter. I know this is not the path of a fine craftsman, or that of a piano builder, but it is rare that you are doing work on a jobsite that is that precise. And, to quote Uncle Jim: "I will do my job so fast that when I finish, and it's wrong, I will still have time to fix it and be finished before the guy who took his time and did it right the first time." I'll admit that there is a time and a place for taking your time and doing it right the first time, but more often than not, guys take their time because they just don't care how long it takes.

I was in White Cap (material supplier) the other day, impatiently waiting for my turn at the counter, and this cashier told the guy he was helping that he was sorry it was taking so long. The guy he was helping said, "I don't mind, I'm getting paid by the hour." After he said that he turned to look at me, I think looking for some validation of his quick wit, and I looked at him disappointedly and just shook my head. What I took his response to mean was, 'I don't mind because I don't like my boss and I don't care if he has to pay me to stand around and waste my time. I also don't give a crap about our client who is probably paying for this, and I couldn't care less about my coworkers who probably rely on my help to make their work more efficient. In fact I don't care about myself nor our society at large and I want to see all of it go down the toilet.' Maybe it's always been there, and I just now am noticing it, but I think that attitude is becoming more and more common. Then again, maybe I was just having a moment.

When you are at work and you look at the clock and it says 1:30 p.m., you can react in only two ways: 1. "Holy Jesus, it's only 1:30. Last time I looked it was 1:25. Is that clock broken? How am I going to find the intestinal fortitude to make it to the end of this shitty workday?" Or: 2. "Goddamnit! How the hell is it already 1:30?! I am never going to finish what I wanted to finish by the end of today."

If you don't find yourself in the second category, it is your duty as a man (if you are a man) to stand up right now (if you are reading this at work) and walk over to your boss and give her your two weeks' notice. I'm not saying you need to be in love with digging ditches or sanding drywall, but if you've gotten to the point where you are staring at the clock, wishing it would all just end, or would rather be standing in line at White Cap, then it is time to make a change. There has to be something else out there that is worth your time.

After about a year of struggle, it was becoming harder and harder to resist the juggernaut that was the huge house project. That job was a classic case of a client not understanding how changes to the original plan would cost more money and take more time. It became harder and harder to answer questions about why the job was taking so long or costing so much when the answer was always in the same key of, "Well, the 'crew' is busy working on ______ that was not part of the original scope." Nonetheless, I persevered and kept at it—trying as I could to move the project towards a completion goal that seemed to keep moving further and further away from me.

While only topping out at a mere 7,500 square feet, my project turned out to be too much for one man to handle. In order to do that job the way it needed to be done, I would have needed at minimum two more people working for me. First, a bookkeeper to handle all documentation of contracts and orders, track all expenses, and handle the hours/payroll of the "crew" (astonishingly, I was in charge of payroll too). And second, I would have had a skilled builder working for me as a superintendent, who could show everyone on the "crew" how to actually build things correctly so that I wasn't bogged down in the minutia of minor building details like how to properly glue PVC pipe or the best technique for taping the reinforced plastic sheeting in the crawlspace, to name just two examples of time-sucking tasks that were necessary when working with an entirely inexperienced group of hillbillies. But, of course that was not in the cards, and in the end I was fired from the job. I chalk it up to a basic system breakdown which I could have anticipated and possibly prevented if I were more experienced when the project began. If I had it to do over again, I would not have been so cavalier about how much man power it was going to take to execute that job correctly.

Because in the trades you are directly accountable for everything you do, good and bad, it is easy to get fired. If you don't do what you say you're going to do for a client, they will fire you. If you are an employee and you screw up bad enough on a job, you can bet they will fire you. There is a direct accountability that is built into the trades that is actually kind of beautiful. You are your own man in the trades. When you do well, it is obvious, and when you screw up, you have no one to blame, no team to hide behind, just you and your stupid stupid stupid self! I have been fired a bunch of times, and every time I more or less deserved it.

Despite the obvious frustrations that I had with that job, I learned a new way (new to me at least) to operate a design-build firm—where the client acts as their own general contractor, and I act as designer and project manager. This "new way" has since saved my clients boatloads of money, and I have found has the potential to actually build a better product. Working now solely as designer and project manager, I charge my clients on a T&M basis for my design and managerial services. They in turn agree to be involved in the project to varying degrees; some less involved than others, but involved nonetheless. The client, as owner-builder, is the contractor of their own project, and I help them find and hire subcontractors who they then contract with directly. The advantage of this process is that they get design-build, but they don't pay any general contactor's markup (which can be upwards of 25%) on everything from material to labor and subcontractors fees. Depending on the client's level of involvement, they can use my supervisory services as much or as little as they want.

Every cloud has a silver lining. Had I not had that giant project draw me away from my other job, I would not have ventured out on my own again, and I am very happy that I did.

In the end I am grateful for that job, even though it still gives me work-mares.

CHAPTER 17

Uncle Jim's three rules of plumbing (pretty sure he plagiarized these):
1. Shit flows downhill.
2. Payday is on Friday.
3. Never put your fingers in your mouth.

It's a cliché as old as lead pipes, but it's true: shit does indeed flow downhill. It is astonishing how often you encounter drain pipes that have an uphill section (or two). It's possible that things buried in the earth move over time due to roots, earthquakes, poltergeists, what have you, but it's also possible that those pipes were laid by someone who didn't know how to cost effectively solve the problem that they were faced with. It's possible that they had a rock in their way and no heavy equipment, so they just said, "well it's only uphill for a couple feet." Don't do that; you have to figure out how to make the pipes slope downhill—the whole way.

Problem solving is an essential skill for anyone in the building industry. Maybe success in any industry requires problem solving; I bet problems arise in every line of work. I don't know what it is like to have to solve problems in corporate management, or in high-tech, but for a contractor, you either solve problems or you have to pay for your client's remodel (or you can always move and change your phone number). The instinct develops in the contracting arts to be extremely creative in avoiding problems.

I should point out that this can be taken too far. We used to work with this guy named Deano who would go out of his way to do things to outsmart the building inspector. His catch phrase was, "You don't need those (fill in the blank), they don't really do anything." For example, one time we were framing a very tall room that was an addition to a house, and part of the structure was a steel "bucket" which served the function of attaching a very large beam to a very large post. Deano's idea was to not actually fasten the bucket to the beam, but:

Cut the bolts off so just about a half inch was left.

Sharpen that remaining half inch into a point.

Hammer the bolts into the holes in the bucket—just enough so they would stick and make it seem like the full bolts had been installed.

Then the inspector would come and look at our work and assume that we had actually bolted the bucket to the beam.

"Yeah, and then after he's gone we just have to pop the bolt heads out," said Deano.

"And why would we want to do that?" asked Matt.

"That way your drywaller doesn't have to notch the drywall around all of those bolt heads that are sticking out. You see, you don't need those bolts. They don't actually do anything," Deano would say in a low tone, as if he had uncovered a building conspiracy.

"You want me to not bolt the beam into the bucket and totally trick the building inspector for the benefit of our drywaller?" asked Matt in all out wonder. "I think the drywaller is going to figure it out!"

Deano's visionary work-arounds were at their core just problem solving. He got a little carried away with the impulse, and he eventually began solving problems that didn't need solving. I even think he created problems out of thin air because he knew he could come up with some brilliant solution—and he would. Ultimately, Deano created too many problems and I had to stop calling him. I still have a very soft spot in my heart for the guy, though. He was all heart. If you asked Deano for something, he would give it to you without question. He was the kind of guy who would give you his truck if you needed it, or money if he had it, and would go out of his way to help you if you needed help. I miss working with the man, but in this business it's hard enough to make money hiring normal, predictable people—guys like Deano will drive you to drinking (at breakfast).

Nonetheless, problem solving is an essential skill. So many unknowns exist at the beginning of a project that you are bound to get into some tricky situations even if you don't make any mistakes. Of course, you will make mistakes; it's just inevitable, and the best you can do is efficiently fix your mistake. Usually, fixing the mistake is best solved by just tearing everything out and doing it over again. However, that doesn't mean you shouldn't try and come up with a clever way to fix your mistake quickly and with as little energy output as possible. Just make sure that you are keeping track of how much time you are investing in the fix.

One time when I was working in San Francisco for Dave #2, I cut a fairly odd shaped piece of drywall to go on a ceiling and I accidentally drew the mirror image of the shape, so it came out upside down. Well, I just decided to put it on the ceiling with the wrong side out. Who cares? It's paper on both sides, right? Your drywall guy will tell you there is a difference. I guess one side is meant for taping and texturing and blah blah blah, and like a junior Deano I knew whatever problem I was creating I was smart enough to fix it. So, Dave #2 comes into the hallway and looks at what I did and says, "Is that going to work?"

"Yeah, don't worry, it's nothing we can't handle with a little

HOT MUD!" I said (singing that last part).

He responded with more than a little doubt in his singing voice, "And then maybe a little BONDO?"

And then Matt came around the corner and put the whole thing into perspective by singing, "Or you could just take it down and put up the right size DRYWAAAALL!" What a dick.

He was right, though. It's counterintuitive, but usually the more efficient solution to an issue in building is just to take everything apart and start from a point where you have a clear perspective. Sometimes you just need to gut an entire room rather than try to cut holes in the drywall here and there and try to snake wires from one hole to the other like you're ice fishing.

Speaking of drywall: Another of Jim's favorite things to refer to was "shit-house luck." I don't exactly know what shit-house luck was, but essentially he was saying that it's always better to be lucky than good. One time I was driving down Gough Street in San Francisco and I had about four sheets of drywall in the back of my 1993 Ford Ranger. I had the tailgate down for whatever reason—maybe to add more length to my six foot bed—but the effect was that the drywall was not as securely loaded into my truck as it should have been, and going around a right-hand turn I lost all four sheets onto one of the busiest streets in the city. As you may know, drywall is pretty brittle, so I was sure that I had destroyed the whole load, but couldn't just leave it on the road, so I took three rights and came back to the pile in the road. To my astonishment, not only had no one run them over, they were barely scratched. I guess the way they sailed out of the back of my truck, they landed on top of a cushion of air and gently alighted on the street. I quickly jumped out of my truck, loaded them back in, and drove to the jobsite. I'll take lucky over good any day.

I've lost a lot of shit out of the back of my truck over the years, and I don't feel good about it. I always have tried to be a courteous hauler of goods. I've lost plywood and nearly caused an accident, and I know I've lost screws and nails. Any time I see a screw or nail in the road or in a driveway I pick it up and properly dispose of it just to try and balance out the karma that I clearly have coming to me from my years of truck bed detritus (incidentally, that is also going to be the name of my new classic rock/country band).

One of my earliest jobs was selling and delivering furniture at a company called Underground Furniture. Even back then, my boss Corey would tell me, "If you lose a piece of furniture out of the back of the pickup, don't stop." I never felt good about that policy, so I always turned the rear view mirror so I wouldn't be able tell if anything flew out of the truck. I just didn't want to be in the position of having to lie about a sofa spinning across five lanes of traffic and taking out a minivan. I would just pull up to the delivery and look to see if we still had all the things in the truck that we left the shop with.

I don't lose much out of my truck these days. Of course, I still make mistakes. What has changed is my ability to solve the problems that arise. I lose less sleep than I used to and I think it is because I have come to trust my own capacity to problem solve. I tell myself, 'Self, this is the time for sleep. Whatever you're thinking about can wait until the morning.' And for the most part, it works. I've become more and more comfortable with the notion that shit happens, and even the most experienced, well-trained, well-managed crews are going to make mistakes, and then solve them to a degree that no one will ever know the difference.

When I was young, I remember driving over the Golden Gate Bridge and thinking it was perfect. I never was able to conceive of men actually assembling or fabricating parts, and just figured the bridge had always been there. Anyone who has ever traveled over the Golden Gate Bridge knows how easy it is to be awestruck by the beauty of the thing. It reminds me of a church with its steeple towers, and the curtain cables that that are at once both massive and delicate. The walls created by the cables give the space a feeling of ascendance into the heavens, and of course the fact that the bridge is usually enveloped in clouds doesn't hurt the metaphor. The color, which according to both Wikipedia and Google (exhaustive research going on here) is officially an orange vermilion called "international orange," is elegant and timeless and just perfect. I have had more than one client choose the same color for portions of their projects not only as a reference to the bridge, but also because it is truly a great shade of orange. So there you are, driving over the mesmerizing Golden Gate Bridge, and it looks like God himself placed it in its spot, and you can't even conceive of mere humans designing and building it, but that is in fact who did the work (albeit not without some obvious divine inspiration).

It goes without saying, then, that there were mistakes made in the construction of the Golden Gate Bridge. I don't know specifics (the proper impulse is to fix mistakes, not record them for prosperity), but undoubtedly there were pieces that were designed incorrectly and didn't fit, steel that was fabricated inaccurately in the steel shop, holes that didn't line up for some of the 1.2 million rivets, and pilings that were off layout by a tiny amount. In all of those cases, men (no women were involved in the life-threatening work on the bridge) figured out a solution to make the thing work.

I recently watched a show called *Mega Structures* or *Super Structures*, or something like that, and they were exhibiting the building of an enormous bridge in Southeast Asia. The bridge was an asymmetrical, twisting, writhing form that was pure art. The complexity of the shape was only possible to construct with the aid of computerized manufacturing techniques and computerized drafting. Without the most advanced technology available today, the bridge would not be buildable; yet even with all of the advanced technology, human beings still had to put the pieces together.

In this show, the foreman in charge of the build was a guy from South Africa. He had an office about the size of mine (it's small), and he had a bunch of guys working under him who ranged in skill from laborer to highly skilled journeyman. Most of them did not speak English, the foreman's language, so communication was challenging, but they set about to build this bridge. They looked at the plans, and they prepared the site, and then they poured concrete for the pilings just like you do for a house—only with the added difficulty of doing it under water.

Finally, they lifted the premanufactured pieces into the air to begin bolting the enormous structure together to create the shape of the bridge. But guess what? Some of the pieces didn't fit. So, they got out their torches and welding equipment and modified the enormous premanufactured pieces so that they would fit the "actuals" that existed in reality. This might not seem crazy to you, but watching this on this TV show was nothing short of an epiphany for me. Even in these mega structures that seem so big and complex that only the most flawless and perfect technology could create, there were mistakes made. Mistakes were made and people figured out a way to fix them right there on the jobsite. Boom—mind blown.

As a way of paying as little "tuition" as she can, a good builder must be constantly in the mode of avoiding mistakes and solving problems before they arise. That is not always possible, but it is the ideal. Not all problems are physical mistakes like incorrectly framed window openings, or equipment accidentally crunching brand new siding on a house. Sometimes problems arise in estimating job costs, and you are forced to come out of your pocket to pay for a client's stuff.

If I have bid a job and made a mistake like ordering the wrong size window, for example, it is really hard to go back to a client and ask for more money, and it is very easy for a client to say no. Usually windows take a long time to order and are totally custom, so cannot be returned. Additionally, by the time you realize a window is the wrong size, the building has likely already been framed and sheathed in plywood. Solution: Eat the cost of ordering a new window and take the incorrect window to your house to use in your Winchester-mansion-of-a-greenhouse that you are one day going to build (or your wife promises to call a hauling company and send all your stored building materials to the dump).

I said it before, but it is worth reiterating: in an attempt to provide the lowest costs possible to my clients, I have often made the mistake of being seduced by the bottom line. There is such a temptation to keep the bid low that you can often "cheat" on your prices, even though you know you are cheating yourself in the end. This temptation must be avoided at all costs. It is better to miss out on a job than be imprisoned by a job which you are never going to make profitable. Many contractors fall into this trap and end up using funds from one job to fill in the gaps on another. It is a classic scenario, and many homeowners have stories about their contractor using the money from their job to pay for someone else's job. My advice to homeowners would be not to go with the lowest bid possible; pay more for a guy with his shit together. My advice to contractors: just bid high, and if you miss out on the job, then go surfing.

Most of the time clients want things as cheap as they can get them, and this is frustrating because 90% of the time, you get what you pay for. There are deals out there for sure, and of course you don't always want the highest-end product available, but you never, ever, ever want the lowest-end. A bid consists of three parts: materials, labor, and overhead/profit. You don't want to hire someone that is using excessively cheap materials because sooner or later, they will fail. Cheap labor is okay, but usually takes expensive labor to supervise so the cheap labor doesn't make more mistakes than is cost effective to fix. Then there is overhead; if you hire a contractor with very low overhead that can be a good thing, but it also means he probably won't have a shop to store tools or do intricate fabrication, he won't have an office manager or bookkeeper—he'll do it all himself, which takes a lot of time, and he won't have a lot of supervisory employees tasked with managing crews. These things all cost money, but are very helpful in running a high-end, efficient building firm. A one-man show will handle most of the clerical duties and supervising himself, and he will be busy. The last part is profit, and I can say honestly that I don't know a lot of wealthy contractors, especially not ones who are operating with very low overhead—those guys are usually more interested in surfing and fishing than they are in being wealthy, and any one of them will tell you that if they had wanted to be rich, they wouldn't have gotten into contracting. So reducing profit for most guys is not an option. I have found over and over again that you get what you pay for. If you cheap out on building materials, or hire total hacks to install them, you will pay for it one way or another.

Sometimes, though, clients want things simply *because* they are expensive. There is a phenomenon where the price of something alone justifies the purchase. Believe it or not, I have missed out on jobs because I didn't bid high enough. All I would have had to do was double my bid and I would have landed the job—tuition.

Once while working for Dave #2, we were installing these Italian cabinets in a house in San Francisco. The cabinets cost

$75,000 and were flat packed and shipped from Italy, so we had to assemble them when they arrived. The cabinets were made of particle board and, in my opinion, were the exact same quality as Ikea or Home Depot cabinets. The only thing that made them slightly higher-end was the finish on them, which was book-matched wood grain. That is, the grain of the wood ran horizontally across all of the doors and drawer and matched perfectly from cabinet to cabinet all the way around the kitchen. They were pretty cool, but in my opinion not worth $75,000. That is about $1,500 per linear foot of cabinet, and this was 2005. My local custom cabinet shop can build me the highest-end cabinet possible with that same finish for $800 per linear foot today.

This client wanted cabinets from Italy, and they actually wanted to spend a fortune on them. I was tasked with assembling these cabinets and attaching the pulls to the drawer fronts and doors. Putting them together was not difficult for a skilled Ikea veteran like myself, but putting the pulls on the fronts was nerve-racking to say the least. To install the pulls, you have to pick a spot and then drill holes in the fronts for the screws to pass through. Drilling holes in $1,500 per foot cabinetry that is perfectly book-matched throughout the entire kitchen is nothing short of terrifying. It is akin to the diamond cutter cutting the world's largest diamond, who upon striking his chisel for the first cut passes out.

Dave #2 came by after I had finished to look at my handiwork, and after he had a brief look around he felt satisfied and we began talking about something else (probably surfing). We were talking for a few minutes when Dave—mid sentence—let out a scream, "Ahhh!" He was looking at the refrigerator, which had book-matched panels as well. Apparently I had misunderstood his instructions on where to put the fridge pulls. I had drilled holes in the center of the freezer drawer when the pull was supposed to be offset. Whoops. Don't worry, though, I didn't need to pay for an entire new set of cabinets. We found someone who artistically filled the holes I had drilled in the wrong place, and we moved the handle into the correct place. Deano would have been proud.

CHAPTER 18

The following is based on an unofficial, unscientific, half-baked survey that Matt and I came up with at our local pub, The Toad in the Hole, one afternoon during a "safety meeting." We each wrote down on the back of a beer coaster a list of subcontractors:

Painter

Carpenter/Framer

Electrician

Plumber

HVAC

General

Concrete Guy

Drywaller

Tile Guy

Then we each wrote down one word to describe the essence of who each of these various subs were. One word to sum up the stereotypical guy who ends up doing the trade on the list. Our lists were nearly identical. So, I decided to take it one step further and pose this same list to all of my builder friends and see what they had to say. Again the lists that came back were very similar. I've ruminated on this trend and I'm not sure I can fully explain why everyone I polled had the same stereotypical view of people who work in the different trades. Could it be that there is something inherent in each trade that repeatedly attracts the same type of person? Or could each respective trade be a force for transformation where an otherwise normal and functioning person is morphed into the stereotype that is that trade? Or maybe we all just work with the same small pool of subcontractors. I have a friend who swears that all painters are crazy because of all of the fumes they get exposed to. That may be right, but then how do you explain drywallers? Clearly more research needs to be done in this field.

If you would like to help me further this important area of study please fill in the workbook as follows:

Painter

Carpenter/Framer

Electrician

Plumber

HVAC

General

Concrete Guy

Drywaller

Tile Guy

Email me your results at survey@kellycowandesigns.com

One trade I forgot to put on the list was roofers, but that's okay because I don't care what anyone says about roofers—to me they are heroes. We should all put black asphalt ribbons on our cars to support them. While fire causes much more damage every year than water, water affects seven times more households each year than fire does, and almost everyone has had to deal with leaks and then the mold and the rot that usually follow. So, when you call a roofer, you are calling a super hero who will swoop in at the last minute and risk his life to save your house from water.

He really is risking his life too—I'm not being hyperbolic here. According to a *USA Today* (clickbait) article, roofing is the fourth most dangerous job in America after logging, fishing, and being a commercial pilot/flight engineer (*USA Today*, "25 most dangerous jobs in America," January 9, 2018). Just the other day, we were trying to keep water out of our unfinished project by covering the bare plywood of our roof with sheets of plastic. This, by the way, never really works. My guy Trevor was up on the roof in the rain, stapling the plastic down and trying not to step on the wet surface, when I heard the unmistakable sound of someone falling and landing on the roof. Then I heard the unmistakable sound of someone sliding down the roof, and I ran around the corner just in time to see Trevor flop sideways onto a pile of lumber that was on the ground. Thankfully he wasn't injured, but he did get lucky, as is evidenced by the fact that 48.6 roofers per 100,000 were injured in 2016, with 101 fatalities and 3,150 total injuries. So go hug a roofer!

It may not have been what initially drew me into the building trades, but I would be lying if I said I wasn't at least partially motivated to stay in the building trades because I thought chicks might find it sexy. I could be overestimating me and my fellow builders' sex appeal, but it is a fact that I have had women tell me on multiple occasions that they loved my calloused hands and rough and ready appearance. They might deny it, but clearly there is something about filth and grime that is a turn on to women. One time while I was still in college, my plumber was giving me a ride to work, and I asked him, "So as a plumber, are you required to wear your pants down low enough to let your butt crack show?" His response was classic, "Maaaaan, I'm part of the new breed of plumbers–big and sexy."

As I said before, every builder has more than enough injury stories to fill a book this size. But nobody has stories like plumbers. I remember telling an electrician once that maybe I would become a plumber: "They make good money, right? I've heard like $85 per hour?"

His response was, "You know plumbers have to wade through human shit every once in a while." Enough said.

I have had my fair share of run ins with shit. It's hard to avoid if you are doing fix-it stuff. Hopefully it's always your own shit, but there was this one time when I was remodeling my friend Eric and his girlfriend's kitchen and only bathroom. On my suggestion they bought a travel trailer to live in during the remodel. They were originally going to rough it without the trailer, but their house had one bathroom and one kitchen—both of which we were completely gutting. So being the good sports that they were, they lived in the trailer for the duration of the remodel.

In order to dump the black water tank from the trailer (that's where the shit gets stored) we hooked up a special macerator pump, which is basically a garbage disposal for shit, and a hose to a clean-out on the sewer system. This allowed Eric to use the bathroom in the trailer as long as he regularly dumped the black water tank. So, after this one particularly long summer's Friday of plumbing and crawling around under the house, Matt and I were sitting on the only piece of furniture left in the place, an old futon, and we were drinking a much-deserved cold one. Eric asked if it was okay to pump his black water tank, and I told him it was, which was incorrect.

It's required with new construction (in most places) to put drain pipes under test so the inspector can see that there are no leaks, and it's not a bad idea to do it in a remodel as well for the same reason. To test the sewer pipes, you plug up the lowest point of the sewer system and fill the vent pipes on the roof with water until they overflow. Since all of the drain pipes and vent pipes are connected, they all fill up with water, and if they stay full after a period of time, you have no leaks. A more gifted plumber would have had a better way to pull this off than I did at that time. Plumbers use all sorts of neat tools like balloons and easy-to-remove plugs because they really do not enjoy being covered in shit. I simply cut the four inch drain under the house and put a rubber cap on it—my plan being to pull it off after my test and let the water run out under the house and absorb into the soil.

So Matt and I are sitting on Eric's old futon and Eric starts his macerator pump, and it's not long before we start to see water dripping out of the pipe we had capped off in the wall where the sink drain used to connect. We both think, 'Huh, that's peculiar, why is water coming out of the drain?' Apparently the cap we put on—probably just to keep sewer gas from coming into the house while we were working—was not on very tightly, and as Matt gets up and walks over to see what it is, it dawns on me just what's happening. I remember it like it was like a slow-motion scene in a movie:

Matt walks across the room to leaking drain.

Camera close up on dripping from nasty old drain pipe.

Matt reaches for the liquid to touch it and then brings his hand to his face to smell the liquid.

Kelly: "NOOOOOOOOOOOO!"

Matt freaks the fuck out.

I had forgotten that I had not removed the cap and reconnected the main sewer lateral. I know, stupid, but I just was kind of burned out after a long week, and I was not all there when I said it was okay to empty the tank. When Eric asked if it was okay to pump his tank, the answer should have been, "No. NO! Absolutely not. Do not pump your tank, unless you want to fill your whole sewer and vent system up with raw sewage."

Nothing goes wrong on a jobsite like it does when it's the end of the day on a Friday. If you ever find yourself about to start something on a Friday and it is after lunch, just go home. It's not worth the risk. It is a scientifically verifiable fact that tasks newly endeavored on Friday afternoon will not go as planned, and will ruin your weekend.

Anyways, there we were processing what had just transpired, and it began to dawn on me that I was going to have to go back under the house and remove the cap on that pipe. The idea we came up with was to remove the cap, align the two sections of pipe, and quickly slide the rubber coupling from one pipe to the other. Picture Indiana Jones in *Raiders of the Lost Ark* switching the relic out for a bag of sand. I had to be lightning quick. This was not made any easier by the fact that I was lying on my stomach in a relatively small crawlspace, but I was confident I could pull it off with little to no leakage.

"One...Two...THREE!" I slipped the cap off the four inch pipe and immediately, with more force than I was expecting, shit-water started gushing out of the pipe. I tried slipping the coupling from one pipe to the other, but the pressure was fighting me and raw sewage was spraying everywhere. The closer I got the coupling to slipping over the pipe, the more forceful was the spray of shit-water; it was like putting your thumb over the end of a garden hose. I was so grossed out that I just started yelling like I was William Wallace storming a castle. Eric, God bless him, was under the house helping me (from a safe distance), and eventually we got the coupling in place. I still feel dirty from that experience.

Being dirty is kind of a constant state of affairs in the trades. No matter what you do to a house, it creates dust. It's just inevitable. I have yet to adequately convey this message to my wife, who sees the plastic and the tape and all of the measures I go to in order to keep dust from migrating out of the kitchen remodel and into the rest of the house, and assumes that it is going to work. It never works. Not entirely at least. Plastic, fans, tape, and all the stuff you do to mitigate dust only mostly works. Dust has a way of getting through. Best approach is just to move out. I have offered many a client a rebate to use on a hotel if they agree to move out during a remodel, especially during the demolition phase.

There is a temptation to live through a remodel and endure the stress of cooking in a makeshift kitchen in your garage that no one ever correctly anticipates. I am reminded of a *Far Side* comic where the devil is giving a guy the choice between eternal damnation and living through a remodel, and the devil says, "It's kind of a toss-up, eh?" That is how you should think of it. The only member of the family that is happy living through the remodel, and then totally bummed when it is complete, is your dog.

...

As true as it is that the average tradesperson is not equipped with all the skills needed to fit into society, and therefore "ends up" in the trades, the average homeowner is not equipped to deal with tradesfolk. One of the core functions of a contractor is to provide a buffer between the people doing the work and the people who will be enjoying it. If you hung out with the guys building your house or remodeling your kitchen at lunch you would probably lose your appetite, but then again I've heard some of the most hilarious things while sitting around a jobsite lunch break.

My first experience with how the general public feel regarding dirty tradespeople was before I graduated from

UCSD and I was delivering furniture for Underground Furniture. I was delivering a bed to a woman who was having her whole house remodeled. There were a bunch of trades in the house doing their finish trim, as the project was nearing completion, and while I wasn't supposed to be assembling the bed I decided I would go ahead and do it for the insanely hot older woman (maybe thirty-five?) because I am a nice guy. While I was finishing up the bed assembly, our client, who had been wandering in and out of the bedroom where I was working came up to me and said, "Sorry, but you are the only non-creepy person in the house right now. Would you mind unzipping my dress?"

I couldn't believe it, so of course I said, "Yes."

As she turned around I thought to myself this is it—this is how all great stories that you read in Hustler start. So I began pulling her zipper down at what my nineteen-year-old level of experience calculated was the appropriate speed, slowly but not too slowly, and tried to stay calm as I passed her black bra and then down past her curvy lower back and revealed her black panties, when she snapped around and said, "I said zip *up* my dress!"

I said, "Oh shit, sorry," and very quickly zipped her dress back up. I was so embarrassed I quickly gathered up my stuff and made a break for the door. Before I could leave she thanked me, gave me a tip, and a smiled as I hustled out.

Looking back, I swear her dress was already fully zipped up when she asked me to zip it "up," and she asked me to unzip it just to mess with a nervous nineteen-year-old kid. I hope that was the case, and if so, God bless her.

That gig working in the furniture shop was another job that taught me a lot about work itself. One of the best lessons I learned there was one which I should never have had to learn, but such are lessons. During a long trip to New York, my boss Corey left his wife in charge of the store. I felt like she was always hanging around unnecessarily, poking her nose into our business. I mean, what right did she, wife of the owner, have to know how we were handling her husband's business? We were nineteen- to twenty-year-old men who were clearly more knowledgeable and more responsible than this interloper, right? Ah, what a jackass I was. Anyways, Corey came back from New York about five years too early—before I had matured enough to know not to say exactly what was in my head. I told Corey that next time he went on vacation, he should consider taking his wife with him. Yep, I said that. Corey did not punch me, or even fire me. He being a good twenty years my senior had something called self-control. He slept on that comment and came in the next day and we had a come-to-Jesus moment. I needed that, apparently.

Being a good employee never came naturally for me, and that's probably why I started out on my own so early. Corey stopped short of punching me for my comments about his wife, but my manager in my first restaurant job after high school did not. I was working at a new hip-ish restaurant in Santa Rosa, and I was not taking my manager's critique of my work with much grace. I wouldn't listen to what he was telling me and I actually started giving him shit back when he asked me to follow him outside for what I imagined was a serious reprimand. When I turned the corner by the dumpsters, he socked me right in the stomach, and I doubled over. It wasn't a hard punch, but I didn't expect it, and it instantly snapped me out of my bitchy attitude. He said, "We good?"

And I whimpered, "Yeah, thanks, I needed that." And I did need it. I am a believer in what the Libertarians call the non-aggression principle, but I look back at that sock to the gut as one of the best things that happened to me at that time of my life. Go figure. He and I are still close friends to this day, and I know he feels bad about that incident, but he shouldn't. Sometimes you need a trusted friend to snap you out of a destructive state with something extreme.

Feel how you may about the various trades—we all have our preconceptions—but the work that is done is honest work. What I mean to say is that no amount of bullshit can cover up a door that is out of square, or plumbing that is leaking, or tile that is crooked. You can try bullshitting your client, but it is a sad sight to see, and in the end the proof is in the pudding.

The same goes for employees. Guys who don't perform get exposed quickly, and excuses for failure rarely get any traction. You might think that all painters are drunks, and you might be right, but if the work gets done for time and money that was promised, who can really complain?

CHAPTER 19

"For where your treasure is, there will your heart be also."—Jesus, Holy Bible: King James Version

I have found many a newspaper tucked away in the walls of an old house—sometimes as an early version of insulation and more often just as a time capsule that someone had the foresight to leave behind for the benefit of Futureman. One time I was working on a circa 1910 house deep in the woods above Cloverdale, CA, and when we pulled the wall apart I found two unique time capsules. One was left by Mother Nature herself, and the other by a builder. The former occurred inside the wall where, through a hole in one of the studs, mice were able to get into the stud bay (the cavity inside the wall between two studs—sixteen or so inches apart, and between the drywall/plaster attached front and back), but they could not get back out. The hole by which they entered was too high up in the bay. The bottom eighteen inches of space was filled with a stratification of dead mice. The bottom four or so inches was nothing but skeletons, and nearer the top the mice were less and less in a state of decay with the top layer consisting of whole, newly deceased mice. The creepiest part of the dead mouse time capsule was that somewhere along the way a snake came through the hole—probably going after a trapped mouse, and it came to the same fate as the mice. It is a horrible thought, but I imagine the snake was trapped in there alive for quite a bit longer than the mice, as snakes can subsist on little food for a very long time. That scene, straight out of the Bizarro Smithsonian exhibit, haunts me to this day.

The second unique thing I found in the walls of that same house was a treasure map. The map was folded up and left in an old tin Prince Albert tobacco can. The tin was left lying flat inside the walls, and the side facing up was rusted to the point of not being recognizable (probably due to mouse urine), but the bottom side was in pristine condition. I carefully opened the top and removed the paper inside and found a note that read:

Sept 28-1942

For What You Want

Measure 400 ft due North then 100 ft
South to the big Madrone tree dig 3½ ft
you will find it there

Harry W. Jack

And it was written on the back of this:

Located 2 Miles North of South San Francisco, Bayshore Highway at Brisbane

An actual treasure map! So of course I put down my tool bags and walked outside to locate this madrone tree. There were a couple of problems that kept us from finding this treasure.

The directions say to walk 400 feet due north, and then 100 feet south. Why not just 300 feet north, and then go to the north side of the big madrone? Or, 301 feet north and 1 foot south?

The note was written in 1942. Madrone trees only live about 200 years, so it is possible that the big Madrone was near the end of its life fifty years before I found the note. Also, the hillside in question was covered in madrone trees, so it was not obvious which tree might be the dead madrone, or the live one, or the leftover remnant of the big madrone.

The owner of the house where I was working was reportedly a billionaire, and when I gave him the note he was very grateful, but not very interested in looking for the treasure. I don't know if his being a billionaire meant he didn't need treasure, or he didn't believe in buried treasure, or what his deal was, but he was clearly much more enthused by the map and Prince Albert tobacco tin than he was in finding the actual treasure.

I always try and leave something in the wall now. Burying a time capsule in the wall is the ultimate in delayed gratification. It is not only delayed but detached as well, because you will never experience the discovery of the thing you left. You just get to imagine the joy it will hopefully bring to Futureman.

Chris and I thought it would be a good idea to do a time capsule in the remodel at Barry's house (the place where I cut through the shirts), so we got dressed up like slutty drag queen construction workers and had a photo shoot. We printed a few pictures and put them in the wall with a whole SF Chronicle from that day. I like imagining that the person who discovers the photos is so far in the future that they don't get the joke. They might think, 'Hmmm, workers back in the day were not as concerned about wearing protective clothing.'

CHAPTER 20

"He who is unfit to serve his fellow citizens wants to rule them."—Ludwig von Mises

I have probably had hundreds of interactions with building inspectors over the course of my career, and I have to say I have never gotten comfortable around them. To me they are cops looking to bust you, and no matter how cool they try to be, they are still capable of ruining your day just because they feel like it. If you are not familiar with what they do, building officials are essentially in charge of interpreting building codes, which are cooked up, handed down, adopted locally, and (at times) seemingly made up on the spot by your local municipality. The human beings that are in charge of doing this are subject to all the same whims as the rest of us—anger, greed, ego, hunger, stupidity, general lack of personality, and all the other human characteristics that end up keeping us from being the heroes we always thought we'd be.

Honestly, I think if you removed building officials from the building department, you would find them to be decent, ordinary people. It is not in me to demean or belittle a person solely based on their career choice. I will say, however, that building department employees as a breed are not known for their creativity. Most building inspectors and building department employees—like their counterparts in the DMV or post office—are very "by-the-book-y," and are not capable of looking beyond the letter of the law in order to expedite the building process. Mix that with the little bit of power that they wield and you can have a tyrannical situation. For example: in most cases, when an inspector catches a mistake or an oversight, they want to see it fixed in person, and only the most lenient will accept a photo instead of having to make a return to the jobsite. This makes no sense. Why waste everyone's time and hold up a project by having to return to the jobsite to see something in person, if a photo will suffice? Maybe it is a case of building officials simply not realizing that they are acting in an antisocial way. When you are being paid by other people's taxes and wasting other people's money instead of your own, you tend to see things differently.

Sometimes contractors hang up their bags and go over to the dark side. You will hear a lot of contractors refer to building inspectors as failed contractors, or that they became building inspectors because they couldn't "hack it" as contractors. This could be true. I, for one, think former contractors make the best building inspectors because they understand how things actually get done, and are less prone to getting caught up in the letter-of-the-law approach to code enforcement. Additionally, you have to remember that most contractors can't "hack it" being contractors, so it shouldn't be that surprising to find former contractors doing jobs elsewhere in the building industry—someplace where you won't lose money, get sued, or become separated from any of your fingers. I don't hold any judgment against a person who doesn't find success in the contracting trade; as I have already said, it's fucking hard. These contractor-turned-inspectors are probably the best we can hope for as builders.

Then there are the bad ones who will never cut you a break no matter how insignificant the mistake or oversight. These guys are not going to heaven. We have an inspector here where I live called Scary Larry. He is infamous for checking every little detail in a building and not accepting photos of fixes. He also is known for asking for changes on approved plans because he doesn't believe the engineer did his job correctly. One time he asked us to add plywood to the interior wall of a house because he didn't think the engineer accounted for enough sheer strength in the design. As if all of the calculations and engineering details and stamped and approved plans that we had for the job were not adequate. But in ten minutes of walking around the house, he understood enough to know that we needed more sheer strength in that one wall. This is the action of a tiny tyrant, and how he hasn't been physically assaulted on the job yet (something I absolutely do not condone) I can only speculate.

We have another inspector here called Mark. He is a former contractor, and when he shows up on the jobsite, he uses common sense and trust to help you with your project, not try and show you that he is a powerful person who knows more than you do. If you look like you know what you're doing or he has seen your work before, he will give you the benefit of the doubt. He never lets things slide that are actual mistakes or oversights, but he trusts us, and we trust him; it's almost as if we were grown men acting like adults and sharing a mutual respect.

When you want to build something, the process begins with plans. And, as we all know, even the best laid plans are subject to the laws of the universe, which incidentally, are written on a poster in your local print shop. Because building department employees are human beings, they can differ wildly in their expectations. On occasion I have drawn and submitted plans to the county building department that have come back with zero comments; that is to say that the person working in the building department who was charged with checking the plans to make sure they met the codes and expectations of the county made no comments as to how I needed to change or correct the plans in order to grant us a building permit. On other occasions I have submitted minor sets of plans for small jobs that have come back with dozens of comments. I have even submitted identical plans for modular homes—completely identical except for the location—and they came back with differing comments. Apparently plan-checking is more an art than a science.

Recently I was talking with my old business partner Mike, who works for a big building firm in town, and I was telling him about the new plan checker at the city and what a douchebag this guy was because he gave me back my plans for a minor addition with eighty-seven plan check comments. Eighty-seven! Mike told me that around his office, the record for plan check comments was forty-four. I asked, "Was that on a 400 square foot addition?"

"No, it was a 4,000 square foot house."

Granted, these two cases of plan-checkery were not by the same person, or even the same municipality, but their offices are only five miles apart, and I think we can all agree that they are part of the same system and therefore are expected to operate in similar manners. And yet, somehow the same system that gave me and my engineer zero plan check comments on a 6,000 square foot project saw it necessary to give me and my engineer eighty-seven comments on a project that is less than one tenth the size.

The reason that this occurred, as I see it, is connected to what I was saying before about not training builders properly. Here you have a young guy—trained as an engineer, with all the brilliance his education could provide—but with zero building experience. He was trained to check boxes, but wouldn't know a jobsite from a website. He wouldn't know a jobsite from a hole in the ground! (Get it?) So, just like the laborer who has no formal training in carpentry or electrical work but ends up doing advanced and dangerous work before she's ready and forced to learn as she goes, this plan checker has to learn that he doesn't actually know how buildings get built in the real world by screwing up some poor lady's 400 square foot addition. He has to have me call him and tell him he is being ridiculous, and tell him how things actually work on a job, which is no doubt demeaning (and not actually productive from my perspective), and eventually he'll either figure it out or get himself fired (yeah, right).

...

People are always going to try to get away with what they can in regards to laws and codes—I think that's just human nature. And building departments for the most part have to accept this. The building department should not take an adversarial position to the public, nor should the public assume the worst of building officials. A true partnership *should* be fostered between the two. The city *should* have an easy to use website, and the people working there *should* be trained in good customer service. They *should* keep hours that make it easy to come in and talk to a person. They *should* also strive to approve (or disapprove) your plans in an expeditious manner. At the time of this writing, we are currently dealing with the aftermath of the fires in Sonoma County, and the city of Santa Rosa as well as Sonoma County each have an office set up to deal specifically with fire rebuilds. They guarantee a turnaround of five days from the time you submit your plans until they come back with either comments or approval. Normally the process takes about twelve weeks. I would like these municipalities to explain how they have allowed the process to take twelve weeks when we all now can plainly see that they have the ability to turn permits around in five days.

The building department should treat the public like customers whose business they value, and not like drivers waiting in line at the DMV. For our part, though, as citizens of the cities and counties where we live, we also need to take responsibility for our role in creating the environment that exists in the offices of our respective municipalities. We are, after all, responsible for electing the leaders who create the laws, and in some cases we vote on those laws directly. If you agree with me, stop reading this drivel and go write a letter to your city council representative and tell them you want all building permits to be approved in five goddamn days.

Then again, what if we got rid of the building department all together? What would a community look like if every person were allowed to build their house however they saw fit? I bet it would look the same or better than it does today. After all, building permits didn't even come into existence until the 1960s in most places, and many of the homes built long before then are still standing today. My parents' Victorian was built in the 1860s without any county supervision, and in my opinion it was built better—with better materials, and by carpenters who gave a damn—than most houses that are thrown up in just about every residential development project today. Did the advent of building permits give us better looking neighborhoods? No, no it did not.

It would be an interesting experiment in community development to allow an average, middle-of-the-road, well representative community somewhere in an average, middle-of-the-road town to use the market to control their building standards. Let's say for this experiment that we are in California, and we keep the California building codes in place, but we remove the building department from the equation. Engineers would still need to be hired to engineer safety into buildings, as they always have been. And, if a home gets built in a way that puts people in danger, lawsuits would still be filed to correct such negligence, and the liability for such negligence would fall on the engineer, architect, or builder who screwed up, which is where it falls today anyways. The building department in every California town carries zero liability if they miss something in the plans or in an inspection, which makes one wonder, 'What exactly are they there for?'

In this fictitious Libertown, the average builder would still be liable for all defects for ten years as they are now, and would certainly not want to be sued for building something that could fall down and injure someone. It's likely that a home owner or landlord who didn't want to be sued for endangering lives would hire an engineer to make sure that the house was built to reasonable standards. Homes in Libertown would get built faster and cheaper as well, and I don't think anyone would ever get sued for not having fifteen inches on either side of a toilet (that is a code requirement).

Here is how the process would play out: Robert the homeowner would have an idea: "I think I want to put a granny unit in my backyard." At our local building department in Sonoma County, a granny unit is called an Accessory Dwelling Unit (ADU), but in Libertown you can call it whatever you want. And so, he would google "Design-build in Libertown," and he would find a well-established and highly reputable firm that could design and build his granny unit for a fair price. That firm would set about designing plans that told the builders (the same firm as the designers) how to build the house. They would also provide the service of planning the project so that the new home would fit within the setbacks and other restrictions on height and size as prescribed by the appropriate zoning for Robert's property. If Robert's neighbors didn't want him to build the house where he was building it, or had questions with the setbacks or allowable heights, Robert would only have to refer them to the survey and layout that he had done by his civil engineer. If they still had a problem, they could take him to court, but the building department is not needed in this equation, and all of this stuff happens even when there is a building department involved anyways.

The design-build firm would then tell Robert, "We are not engineers, so we recommend that we have an engineer help us design this building." This is a good idea for the design-builders because the engineer will provide valuable input about how the structure can be built to be safe and to last, but it is also a way for them to insulate themselves from any liability that they might have if anything goes wrong down the road. If the roof caves in during a heavy snow, they can say, "We didn't engineer the roof. That is on the engineer." Of course, the engineer knows this, so she follows all of the strictest standards of the day. She still does the calculations and she still does field inspections. The only difference is that there is not another guy—the building inspector—repeating the exact same steps, wasting everyone's time and money.

Once the plans are complete and the engineer has provided her details to the design-build firm, work can begin. There would be no two to three month waiting period where the building department nitpicks the plans looking for "mistakes" or redundant notes about obvious situations. I once got into an argument (I know, it's hard to imagine) with a plan checker who wanted me to notate on the plans 'TO USE CORROSIVE RESISTANT WIRE MESH W/ MAX ¼" OPENING ON ALL FOUNDATION VENTS OR ATTIC VENTS.'

I said, "Jimmy, you can't even buy foundation vents that don't meet that standard in a store." He said that wasn't the point, but if I didn't put that on the plans, the builder might not put screens over the vents. Really? Thank God he caught that one, or that house might have been built and left with ugly and blatantly obvious gaping holes in the walls.

Okay, so Robert's design-build firm has begun excavating the ground where the granny is going to go, and before they finish digging they have a soils engineer double check that they are going deep enough and that the foundation was designed properly for this particular soil. This helps give the engineer a layer of protection, as he is relying on the expertise of the geologists to make sure the foundation is sitting on solid material. After everyone is satisfied with the digging part, the foundation guys put up the forms and the steel, the engineer inspects their work, and they pour the concrete.

This process continues throughout the building of the home. The builders put everything together based on the designs of the various professionals involved, and the experts come out to inspect the work before it gets covered up. Even things like energy efficiency or water conservation get designed into the home in this same way. You could choose not to implement those standards, but you would run the risk of some environmentally conscious consumer purchasing your house down the road and suing you or your designer or your contractor to correct those features that are required by code.

The experts you hire to design Robert's foundation, framing, insulation, lighting loads, irrigation system, or even his gray water system all come out to make sure his builders are getting it right. This is not an adversarial relationship the way it can be with the building department. Robert hired these professionals and he wants to make sure that the building is going up per their prescription. It is in everyone's best interest that the plans are followed, and that every expert inspects the work they have had a part in designing.

Removing the barriers to building would have a net positive affect on the housing stock of a community. Prices would fall, building would boom, and all of the previously employed building department employees would get hired by the growing building industry. After all, they are experts in the field of building; why wouldn't they make a great addition to any building firm?

CHAPTER 21

"Practice safe design: Use a concept."
—Petrula Vrontikis

My wife Melissa and I might not be the most romantic couple you've ever met. We rarely buy each other Christmas presents. One thing I do make a habit of doing, though, is I make Melissa a heart every Valentine's day. They all are about the same size—maybe twelve inches by twelve inches—and hang on the wall in our bedroom. We've been married for ten years, and there are seven hearts on the wall because I got a late start. One is made of concrete, one of steel, one out of duct tape, a couple out of wood, one lights up and is made entirely of wire, and another is made from a book.

I don't do a lot of actual building in my career these days, so little things like these hearts are an outlet for my need to create something with my hands. For the most part I wear nice clean clothes to work, with the exception of a bit of marking paint that is on a few pairs of shoes from showing other people where to dig. I have reached a point in my career where I can make a decent living without subjecting myself to all of the pain and misery of contracting. It is nice to have an outlet where I can design a weird thing, make it with my own hands, and make someone happy, all in about a day. I can do it easily, and economically, and it has a maximum impact on my marriage and our house. I think it is important for a man to have an outlet like this to show off in a humble way, and in a way that can be disguised as selflessness. I know my wife sees right through my selfless gifts, but it appears that she loves them nonetheless.

When Melissa and I go on vacation, we like to try and not tourorize the place we visit. Maybe it's from my time in Mexico where I was a foreigner in a foreign land, but was able to immerse myself in the culture there and feel more like a resident than a tourist. One way to do that is to visit a place and stay for a long time. One way to afford staying for a long time is to do some work while you are there. The first time Melissa and I visited our friend John in New Orleans, we went there to help him install a beautiful, reclaimed, cypress door that he found in one of New Orleans' awesome salvage yards on the rear of his Garden District Victorian home. After a little examination of the situation, I informed John that his laundry room/porch where the door was going was not in good shape, and so we ended up tearing the back of his house off and adding a whole new and much bigger room, which thereby initiated a kitchen remodel, and turned my one week visit into three. That trip ranks near the top of my list of vacations of all time. I was not there just seeing the sites and checking Vaughn's on Thursday night off my New Orleans bucket list; I was there getting to know the local Ace Hardware, and getting to know Raymond Twickler, the local sheet metal guy and the Bank, one of the mind-blowing historic salvage yards. I can't visit a place and not imagine what it would be like to live there, so give me a working vacation any day over a cross-things-off-the-bucket-list vacation.

New Orleans in most ways is more like Mexico than it is like anywhere else in the US. A lot of people call it the northernmost Caribbean city, a name that, in my opinion, suits the place well. Trying to get stuff done there is a bit like trying to get stuff done in Mexico, only (thank God) without siesta. I should say here that the trip coincided with the one year anniversary of Hurricane Katrina, so New Orleans was not exactly on top of its game, but by all accounts (including my own on various return trips) not much changed from before Katrina to after Katrina in terms of efficiency in the marketplace.

One example of the "laid-back" attitude in New Orleans'

building industry was the time John and I needed a fairly common and simple to find (by California standards) beam hanger to support the upper floor above a wall we removed in his laundry room. But of course, we could not find it anywhere in New Orleans, so we were forced to go with plan B, which was to have it fabricated. This led us on a wild goose chase until we finally ended up at Raymond Twickler's sheet metal and fabrication shop.

Before I tell you about our experience with Twickler, let me first say something about shop attitude that you will encounter no matter where you go in our great country. It is a mindset that is as pervasive as the nudie calendars hanging in these shop's bathrooms. Shop attitude is a checkpoint—only letting the worthy access the services or parts that inhabit the space behind the counter. Some places are worse than others, but for the most part customer service is not a thing in these shops, and most of the time the person helping you has other things they could be doing, and does not give a shit about you or your wild goose chase.

Of course, this all changes once you get to know the people in a shop and you have shown them that you know what you are doing, and you are not there simply because you enjoy wasting other people's time. When you cross this threshold, you are let into the inner circle and will be included in the samurai-level bullshitting that is ever-present (although usually reserved for the area behind the counter). But until then you must walk the gauntlet of affirming your confidence in the situation that has brought you, hat in hand, through the front door of the shop. The worse places will judge you worthy or not based on your clothes. I usually am dressed in nicer clothes these days, but I kind of relish the situation where I have handicapped myself, and armed only with my trade lingo and knowledge of fractions have to break through a checkpoint for the first time.

I was in PACE plumbing supply the other day and a new guy was trying to help me. He had a pretty chipper attitude, but then another more experienced guy came up and took one look at me in my khaki pants and button down shirt–tucked in of course–and interrupted his junior colleague to say, with major attitude, "Are you a contractor?" A reasonable question, as I believe they only sell to contractors, but the way he said it was obviously meant to imply that I was not, and I should shuffle my leather slip-on shoes right out the door that I came in.

"Yes," I responded, giving him my own attitude back, and silently communicating to him, 'Is that all you got?'

He picked up what I was non-verbally saying and responded, "Well, do you have an account?" I don't think I needed one to purchase anything there, but I had him on the ropes and he was grasping at straws.

"Yes," I responded, that time it was a knockout blow; he

dropped all attitude and I was in. Once in, I knew I could be as dumb as I wanted to about what I was looking for and I just spelled out exactly what I was trying to do, and then let them tell me exactly what I needed. A lot of times just being completely humble yet confident will appeal to the humanity in another blue-collar warrior and you will find that you are beyond the checkpoint without much stress.

Anyways, back to Twickler. John and I walk into Raymond Twickler's dilapidated shop; again, this is the first anniversary post Katrina, so the dilapidation was due largely to the shop being tossed by a category six hurricane, but still seemed a bit neglected given that this was a full year later. There was a section of the shop that had no roof, and it looked like there was a battle going on between order and disorder, and disorder had captured a large chunk of territory and hunkered down. We wander deeper into the shop and find Twickler in his office eating a bologna sandwich. John and I say hi and tell him what we are looking for, and he just sits there loudly eating his sandwich and smacking his lips. He doesn't say anything for a minute and we are looking at each other like, 'Uh…is this guy for real?'

Finally, Twickler takes a loud sip from his Orange Crush soda and clears his mouth with more smacking, and says, "You all the lunch bunch, ain't ya?"

"The lunch bunch?" I respond.

"Yep, while everyone else is eatin' lunch, ya'll drivin' around, come in here. You should be eatin' lunch," he says.

John and I just kind of nod our heads and think to ourselves, 'Yeah, I guess we are the lunch bunch.'

"There is always someone gotta come disturb my lunch," he says, and then returns to eating his sandwich. John and I have been driving around all goddamn morning looking for this beam hanger, and now we have found someone who might be able to help us and he is just sitting there eating his lunch and making us watch. Steam was starting to come out of John's ears.

Eventually, having punished us enough for being in the lunch bunch, Twickler puts down his sandwich and gets up to help us with our hanger. I had made a drawing of exactly what we needed, so all we had to do was find the material in the shop, and for Twickler to cut and bend our piece. This was not easy because the shop was in such disarray, and it almost looked like we were going to strike out again when finally, I can't remember which one of us found the one and only piece of thick enough material that would work for the hanger. Twickler sat down at his shear and his break and began working. I was watching him work, and I could tell that something was not quite right with the orientation of the piece, but before I realized he was doing it backwards, it was too late. Twickler looked up at us and said, "I fucked it up."

I thought John was going to trash the place. He was so angry he might have, but the place was already kind of trashed, so I'm not sure it would have sent much of a message. We left with our heads in our hands, and we set off back to his house to come up with plan C. Later that day, we were telling one of John's friends about our experience with Raymond Twickler, and he said, "Oh, I love Raymond." The friend's wife told us that he would go down and hang out with Twickler and shoot the shit at lunch time. Only in New Orleans.

My first experience of New Orleans was of a town that was beat to hell, and the built environment as well as the people seemed pretty exhausted. Windows were missing in Harrah's Hotel, the street cars were not running on St. Charles Street, and there were huge piles of garbage and debris in various locations throughout the city. The City That Care Forgot looked like it might never be remembered the same way again, and there was a lot of talk about the population never rebounding. Despite all of the exhaustion and pessimistic predictions, there was also a warm sense of community in New Orleans. I never got the feeling that people were desperate or so pessimistic that they were going to give up. People in New Orleans strike me as way too laid-back to just throw in the towel—I think quitting must be for busybodies.

I met another builder down there named Bob, who helped John and me with his back-door-replacement-turned-whole-house-remodel. Bob was your typical just-outside-the-bounds-of-traditional-society contractor/builder but with a New Orleanian twist. He was a true devotee of New Orleans culture and filled me in on much of the politics and cultural tides of current day New Orleans. Bob was a smart dude, and well read. He turned me on to the pride of New Orleans media, WWOZ—a very local radio station with worldwide listenership. He knew a little bit about politics, a lot about culture, and even more about building in the Crescent City. What you wouldn't guess about Bob was that he knew anything at all. He was overweight, had a smoke-stained gray beard, and drove a total beater truck. He cursed like a sailor, wore sweat shorts and dirty t-shirts, and probably lived alone. It took getting to know Bob (not something a tourist could hope to achieve) to realize what a gem of a guy he was. He definitely exceeded superficial expectations.

Bob was a good source for what it must have been like to experience Katrina. He didn't evacuate. He told my wife and I stories of what it was like in the lawless after hours of post-Katrina New Orleans. Bob told me that in the morning when he went out to his truck and he found the whole neighborhood underwater, he decided he would be better off swimming down to his truck and salvaging his tools that were still in the back than just letting them disintegrate. The balls that that takes is hardly conceivable to me. Not only was his truck underwater, the water was polluted and murky, and full of God only knows what kinds of creepy creatures. New Orleans is full of weird critters. I don't think I would have done the same. I figure the tools that were hand tools could have waited until the water subsided, and the power tools were done the second the water touched them, but Bob did it out of principal. He probably could have bought new tools and had his insurance (insurance? probably not) pay for most of them, but he felt like it was his duty to save those tools. Bob had a degree from Cornell, and was what my buddy John calls a classic New Orleans dropout. He was part of a class of folks who just came to New Orleans to drop out of traditional society. Sounds like another group of people I know well.

CHAPTER 22

"Designers think everything done by someone else is awful, and that they could do it better themselves, which explains why I designed my own living room carpet, I suppose."—Chris Bangle

I think I designed my first dream house when I was seven years old. Since then I have not deviated much from the path of my design-build life. I've all but given my life to the trade, although I've come close to doing so. In return for my obsessive dedication to the trade, I have physical scars and deep emotional ones too. I've been burned by clients and burned by actual fire, and I've nearly thrown in the towel on more than one occasion. But like a junky trying to white-knuckle-quit heroin, of course I can't quit. I also have a comfortable income to show for my years of experience and effort. It may disappear tomorrow, but for now I can afford to live in a neighborhood where most people don't lock their doors, and I never see homeless people using my hose to bathe or give water to their pet rabbit (multiple occurrences).

I hoped by writing this book I would paint the picture of what it means to be a builder in this day and age, and shed just a little light on who the people are who are creating the built environment that shapes our collective experience of space. I wanted to let you, dear reader, know who the men are that come into your house and crawl around underneath it, and disappear into your attic only to reemerge dirtier than before, and with a story about why your heater wasn't working, or how they figured out what was making your circuit breakers trip every time you plugged in your electric toothbrush.

I hope I pulled back the veil a little bit and gave an identity to the workers you see driving next to you on the freeway with a load of lumber either strapped to lumber racks or sticking out of the back of their hatchback. I hope the civilians who pick up this book are enlightened by it, and that the builders who read it are not insulted.

In doing so, I guess I painted a sort of self-portrait of one eccentric contractor, but then that was the only way a hack writer like myself could think of telling this story. I'm reminded of a self-portrait my dad did once in art school at College of the Redwoods; it was a photo of things that represented who he was at the time. The picture hangs on my wall and is one of my prized possessions. In the frame are his clothes—his western plaid shirt hangs on one corner of the back of a wooden chair; his boots are on the seat of the chair; his vest on the other side of the chair back. In the background is a bookshelf with books that presumably have meaning—*The Writings of Bob Dylan*, *California Yesterday*, and then again, some might simply represent the books he was assigned to read, but never did. The bookshelf does not seem curated; it is a true representation of the literary identity of the subject—warts and all. On the wall is a Jimmy Hendrix poster and next to the bookshelf a Bob Dylan record. A few unidentifiable knickknacks hang out on the bookshelf, and that is about it. His body is not in the frame, and without it the viewer is compelled to think, 'How much of the "self" in a self-portrait is the physical body?' If you take away the body, do you take away the self? Clearly not.

In this book—my own self-portrait—I suppose I have done something in the same vein by telling the stories of all the people who have shaped the portico of my identity. My dad was there at the beginning and sparked my creativity in his workshop; letting me make just about anything I could think of making. Uncle Jim fanned the flames of curiosity, and Pete Perisic, my first professional mentor, showed me that art and design were not just important in principle but could be my life. Only by the grace of God was I able to cobble together a career out of the strange brew of professional and cultural experiences that I have had up until this point. Dave and his crew of wingnuts, Pancho and his Mexican ingenuity, my former partners Mike and Matt each with their own brand of neurosis, Gay Chris and the lost drag queen photos, Dave #2 who taught me to put surfing ahead of work, Corey from Underground Furniture to whom I still owe an apology and a handshake for suggesting he take his wife with him on his next vacation—all left their mark on me and shaped me into the man and practitioner of design-build that I am today.

Of course I should include all of the clients that I have had both the pleasure and pain to work with over the years. It's tempting to list my clients in order from best to worst—something I've done with Matt in the past, but I think that would be a bit too crude, even for me. Suffice it to say, there were great clients like Jeff with the bike shop, and there were evil clients like Susan and Steve who tried to fleece me out of thirty grand, and François who tried for another $13,000. I nearly threw in the towel at more than one point, and if not for the love and mutual respect of some of my best clients, I probably would have. As bad as the worst clients were, though, they undeniably made me a better builder. Iron sharpens iron.

So here I am today, actually making a comfortable living off of ideas in my head, and by putting my years of experience to work helping people build their dreams.

Somehow all of the weird shit that I got into over my life in the trades has paid off. All of the close calls and mistakes. And, if I had it to do over again...I'd go to law school.